Every Day a Good Day

Every Day a Good Day

Establishing Routines in Your Early Years Setting

Stephanie Shimmin and Hilary White

Paul Chapman
Publishing

First published 2006

Paul Chapman Publishing
A SAGE Publications Company
1 Oliver's Yard
55 City Road
London EC1Y 1SP

SAGE Publications Inc
2455 Teller Road
Thousand Oaks, California 91320

SAGE Publications India Pvt Ltd
B-42, Panchsheel Enclave
Post Box 4109
New Delhi 110 017

Library of Congress Control Number: 2006904535

A catalogue record for this book is available from the British Library

ISBN-10 1-4129-2359-X   ISBN-13 978-1-4129-2359-0
ISBN-10 1-4129-2360-3   ISBN-13 978-1-4129-2360-6 (pbk)

Typeset by Pantek Arts Ltd, Maidstone, Kent
Printed in Great Britain by Cromwell Press Ltd, Trowbridge, Wiltshire
Printed on paper from sustainable resources

Contents

About the Authors

Stephanie Shimmin has run her own nursery school for over 30 years. She is a graduate of the University of Toronto and has a diploma from an early years training college. Her work has included supporting students and newly qualified practitioners, establishing parent links and managing all aspects of the early years setting. She has also lectured and tutored students in an early years training establishment.

Hilary White is a freelance writer and educational consultant living in Somerset. She has a BA Hons in English Literature from Bristol University and a PGCE from Redland College. She taught in both the primary and the nursery sectors and lectured for many years at an early years training college. She has written a number of books in the fields of creative development and communication, language and literacy and is a regular contributor to various early years publications. She has a particular interest in the picture book and has spent a number of years researching its role in the young child's learning and development.

How to use this book

Working with young children is one of the most rewarding, important and challenging jobs you can do. Whether you are establishing routines, creating a supportive and stimulating environment or responding to the many different personalities of the children, there are a seemingly endless number of day-to-day tasks and responsibilities for the early years practitioner. This book sets out to offer some support in these areas. If you can sort out the 'fundamentals' of your setting, everything else should follow on effortlessly.

There is no magic formula for creating the perfect early years setting. There are, however, a number of ideas, approaches and routines that you can try in the ever-evolving task of running your setting. Perhaps you want to re-organize your snack time routine, increase the children's access to the garden or explore different ways of responding to disagreements. Check the relevant chapter in this book and try out some of the suggestions.

The term 'early years setting' covers many different types of establishment for the three to five age group. You may work in a privately run nursery school or a nursery class attached to a maintained primary school. You may be based in a large urban day-care centre or run a small village playgroup. Given that every setting is unique, the ideas, routines and suggestions in this book are described in general terms. They may work for you as they stand, or you may need to adapt an idea to suit the unique nature of your setting. Always bear in mind that the most successful practitioners are able to take the kernel of an idea and make it their own. Whenever you introduce something new, observe the children closely and adjust your approach until it works for you, your children and your setting.

Who is this book for?

This book is aimed at anyone who works in a Foundation stage early years setting.

■ **Students**: if you are a student practitioner, this book will give you lots of tips and techniques to try out during your practice; for example, the practicalities of planning group activities, managing behavioural challenges, supervising mealtimes or helping children with basic routines such as hand-washing. If you are working towards a National Vocational Qualification (NVQ) in any aspect of childcare, this book may also help you provide evidence for your portfolio.

- **Inexperienced practitioners**: if you are a newly qualified practitioner, this book will offer lots of ideas and approaches to help you develop your practice. Although you will not be responsible for overall management, you should be involved in planning and decision making. Having an overview of the early years setting is always useful, and this book will give you some idea of the breadth and range of organization that goes into running a pre-school group.

- **Setting managers and experienced practitioners**: if you are an experienced practitioner, or establishing a new early years setting, this book will give you various ideas to try and sample routines to compare with your own practices. The book also makes a useful reference to lend to new staff and students.

What is included in each chapter?

Each chapter is divided into three broad areas (see contents page). Each chapter also contains **Information Links**, **Curriculum Guidance** and **Case Studies**.

Information Links

The book looks at a number of topics from different angles – for example, you will find information on responding to anger or aggression in Chapters 1, 2 and 6. Where this is the case, the 'Information Links' text boxes will direct you to other relevant sections in the book.

Curriculum Guidance

Everything you do in the early years setting helps to fulfil the **Curriculum Guidance for the Foundation Stage** (QCA, 2000), whether you are talking through a disagreement, showing children how to pour a drink or planning a 'child-friendly' cloakroom. The 'Curriculum Guidance' sections demonstrate how different routines, approaches and ideas meet the requirements of the Stepping Stones and Early Learning Goals. Each Stepping Stone is coded with its colour and the initials 'ss'. Each Early Learning Goal is coded with the initials 'ELG' and codes are also used to indicate which of the six Areas of Learning the goals come from:

PSED – Personal, Social and Emotional Development;

CLL – Communication, Language and Literacy;

KUW – Knowledge and Understanding of the World;

MD – Mathematical Development;

PD – Physical Development;

CD – Creative Development.

Case Studies

Case studies have been included throughout the book to illustrate various different scenarios and situations. Each case study is based on a real event, although the names of both children and adults have been changed to protect their identity. The case studies also include a summary to highlight what they show in terms of both good and bad practice.

Further Reading

At the end of the book, there is a reading list. If you want more in-depth information on areas such as garden play, observation, toileting or any other topic covered in the book, this is where you will find suggestions for useful titles.

Special needs

Supporting children with special needs is an essential part of your role and responsibility as an early years practitioner. Apart from the value of inclusion for all children, you may find yourself in breach of legislation if you refuse to accept a child based on disability and/or special needs. It lies beyond the scope of this book to look in depth at special needs provision. However, where appropriate, there are general references to the importance of supporting children with special needs, observing their progress and adjusting your provision to better meet their requirements. For anyone who requires more detailed information, the Further Reading list at the end of this book includes titles on the autistic spectrum, dyspraxia, AD/HD, supporting special needs in general and writing and implementing Individual Education Plans.

The importance of observation

Throughout the book, you will find **Observation Notes**. These sections highlight some of the most important elements to look out for, linked to the different topics covered in each chapter. They also include relevant points from the **Foundation Stage Profile** assessment scales (QCA, 2003).

Observation and assessment are central to everything that you do in the early years setting. It is observation that tells you what levels children have reached in all aspects of their learning and development; what provision they need in order to progress; how the group is functioning as a whole and whether or not your setting is supporting or hindering the children. Having taken observations, it is essential that you then assess what you have seen, in order to match your provision to the needs of the child. Your observations should also be at the core of record keeping and completing the Foundation Stage Profile.

When making observations, it is important to distinguish between **summative** assessment and **formative** assessment. **Summative** assessment summarizes what level of development the child has reached at a given moment. It is useful for record keeping and providing information for parents' reports. **Formative** assessment informs you of what the child needs in order to progress. Formative assessment should always be at the basis of targeted provision in the early years setting.

Observation and assessment are complex procedures and there are many different methods and approaches.

- ■ **Targeted observations**: these are planned observations where you watch a particular child and note down as much information as possible. It is essential to stand back and not become involved during a targeted observation. Let colleagues deal with any incidents so that you can remain focused on your observation. Many books recommend observing for 5 to 15 minutes, but if you can manage longer, you will gain a much more comprehensive profile. Aim to observe each child in the setting at least once a term. You can also use targeted observation if you have a particular concern about a child and need to gather information. Try to be as neutral as possible; write down the facts of what you see and hear, rather than your subjective judgement. Once the observation is complete, analyze your notes and look for patterns of behaviour, how the child relates to other children and adults, how independently the child operates within the environment, levels of concentration and demonstration of skills and knowledge in all six Areas of Learning.

- ■ **Tracking**: 'tracking' is a form of targeted observation. It can be particularly useful for gathering information about a child who has difficulty settling or engaging with activities. Make a plan of the setting and observe the child during a free choice activity period. Note what they are attracted to and how long they spend on each activity. Always remember that the purpose of tracking is not to 'prove' that a child's behaviour is negative, but to look for ways in which you might support that child.

- ■ **Incidental observations**: incidental observations are little snippets of information that you pick up throughout the day. They can include anything that might be useful to add to the child's record, such as a child engaging with a particular activity or one child helping another. Keep a block of post-it notes™ close at hand so that you can write down anything of interest and stick it straight into the child's records.

- ■ **Observing routines and areas of the setting**: observe the children as they participate in routines such as hand-washing, laying tables for lunch or using the painting easel. How well do they cope with these routines? If they are struggling, what adjustments might make the routine more manageable? Plan to observe each area of the setting throughout the year. Look out for the most and least popular activities, and whether the children are able to use the area independently. Based on your observations, you can then adapt the area to make it more 'child friendly' if necessary.

Choosing when to make your observation is another important consideration. If you have planned a targeted observation because a child is unsettled at the start of the session or having difficulties in the garden, you will obviously need to choose the relevant time and place. For more general observations, aim to observe during a range of situations, including:

■ free choice activity time, both indoors and outdoors

■ planned large and small group activities

■ regular routines such as lunchtimes, hand-washing or getting ready to go home.

This is just a brief summary of some of the main observational methods you can use. For more detailed information on observation, assessment, record keeping and the **Foundation Stage Profile**, see Further Reading.

Settling new children

Welcoming new children into the setting is an essential part of the practitioner's role. From organizing preliminary visits to handling separation anxiety, a well-managed start to children's early years experience can have an enormous influence on all aspects of their lives.

The chapter is divided into three sections:

- Preliminary visits

- The first few weeks

- Handling children's reactions.

Preliminary visits

Preliminary visits give new children a taste of the setting, before they start on a permanent basis.

Dates and timings

When planning your preliminary visits, the first step is to decide the following:

- dates for the visits

- how many to have

- whether to choose mornings, afternoons or a combination of both.

Ideally, the visits should be as close to the child's starting date as possible. The more visits you can arrange, the more opportunity children will have to become familiar with their new environment. However, the needs of the visiting children do have to be balanced against the needs of your established group. If staff find that preliminary visits are disruptive to normal routines, you may prefer to offer just one or two.

Deciding whether to hold visits in the morning or afternoon will depend on how your setting is structured. If you can offer parents* a choice, along with a range of dates, it will help them to schedule the visits into their busy lives. Staggering the dates so that the children are not all visiting at once can be less overwhelming for everyone; it will also enable staff to spend time with each child and their parent.

Another option is for a practitioner to visit the child at home. This can help the practitioner to form a relationship with the child in the security of their own surroundings. However, home visits are only worthwhile if both the practitioner and the child's parents are comfortable with the arrangement. If you try this approach, be certain that your visit is genuinely welcomed by the child's family.

TRY THIS

Toddler groups

Weekly toddler groups give children a long-term opportunity to become familiar with the setting. To run a toddler group, you will need the following:

- a 'spare' practitioner to run the group
- a suitable space
- appropriate toys/books/equipment
- planned activities such as story/singing/craft
- refreshment facilities for children and adults
- insurance and information from the Pre-school Learning Alliance to ensure you are meeting regulations for the under-threes.

Planning the visit

As with any aspect of the early years setting, the preliminary visit needs careful planning. A session of about 90 minutes will give you long enough to offer a variety of different experiences, without overloading the children. Within this timeframe, you can also arrange for the children to arrive after the rest of the group have settled, and leave before lunchtime or home time.

Try to include as many normal, everyday routines as possible. Where necessary, tailor routines to meet the particular needs of your young visitors. For example, you might plan for staff to greet the children and their parents at the front door, rather than your normal practice of having children come directly into the cloakroom. You should also double-check whether any of the visiting children have special needs. Discuss children's

* Throughout this book, the term 'parent' is used to mean any adult who takes responsibility for the child's care outside the setting, including foster parents, guardians, childminders, nannies and grandparents.

requirements with their parents to ensure that you will be meeting their needs during the visit.

The following timetable provides a model for a morning visit. It offers a variety of everyday experiences, along with a balance of adult and child-initiated activities:

- **9.30 – arrival**: greet children and parents at the front door. Show the children their pegs and show the parents the toilets. Invite everyone into the setting.

- **9.45 – free choice activities (approx 45 minutes)**: have ready a selection of activities that the children can respond to at their own level. For example:

    - modelling clay

    - tray puzzles

    - easel painting

    - sticking activity

    - drawing with wax crayons

    - construction toys

    - threading

    - sand and water play

    - the home corner.

    During this period, the children's prospective key workers should aim to spend individual time with each child. If a few children need direction, hold a short, impromptu group, choosing simple activities such as well-known nursery rhymes.

- **10.30 – large group activity (approx 10 minutes)**: invite the visitors to join the group, plus some or all of the other children. Include activities such as story (preferably using a big book) and familiar nursery rhymes. Use children's names as often as possible and sing a 'naming' song (see *TRY THIS – naming songs*, page 10).

- **10.40 – snack time/outdoor play**: check for food allergies before offering snacks. Use outdoor play as an opportunity to chat with parents about their child's visit and introduce parents to one another (all staff need to be clear about who is talking to parents and who is interacting with and supervising the children).

- **11.15 – departure**: departing from the outdoor play area without returning to the setting is a straightforward way for the children to end their visit. This arrangement also enables parents to leave at their own pace, allowing them to chat with one another or let their children play in the garden. Make sure the children are given any drawings or story sacks to take home.

This model can either be adopted as it stands, or adapted to fit in with your particular routines and way of working. For example, you may choose to start the session by gathering everyone on the carpet, introducing staff and giving each new child a name badge. You may prefer to introduce the activities to small groups of children, rather than having a free choice time. How you structure the visit is less important than making sure that the children have a happy and reassuring experience of the setting.

TRY THIS

Story sacks

Borrowing a story sack gives the children a link with the setting once their visit is over. Make up several sacks containing:

- picture book
- toy/game linked to the book
- paper/coloured pencils
- cassette of children singing nursery rhymes made during a visit
- information sheet with tips for using the story sacks.

Invite parents to take a photograph of their child during the visit (use a digital camera for instant results). Slip the photograph into the sack.

Observation notes

During preliminary visits, your main role is to link with the children, rather than make formal observations. It is also worth remembering that the children are not in a 'normal' situation and may react quite differently when they join the setting on a permanent basis. Having said that, you may pick up on some interesting little snippets of information. Make a quick note of anything that seems relevant and share your observations with colleagues.

- Observe how the children respond to the various experiences you offer. Do they engage with activities independently or stay with their parent? Do they link willingly with staff and other children? Such observations can give you an idea of how much support a child will need when they start properly at your setting.

- Look out for different personality traits. Although it is essential not to label children, you can get a sense of the various little characters you will be dealing with.

- Look out for any signs of special needs, such as delayed speech development or co-ordination difficulties. Although you need to be flexible over these first impressions, they may indicate the need for extra support in the future.

- As a team, evaluate your observations and impressions of the visit and look into ways of improving your provision for the future. For example, did parents seem to understand your procedures, or should they be given more information prior to the visit?

For a summary of different observational approaches, see page 4.

TRY THIS

Nursery rhymes

Ask parents to let you know their child's favourite nursery rhymes so that you can sing them during a group session. Tell all the children that you are going to sing 'Baa baa black sheep' because it is Conor's favourite nursery rhyme. Alternatively, give parents a copy of the rhymes you plan to sing so that they can share them with their child before the visit.

TRY THIS

Naming songs

Naming songs are a fun way to introduce new children. They also help visiting children to feel a part of the group. Try the following:

Sing to the tune of 'Peter Pointer'':
    Annie, Annie, where are you?
    Here I am, here I am (child stands up)
    How do you do?
Ask parents to help visiting children stand up and sing: '*Here I am …*'

Clap to the rhythm:
    Joe, Joe, Joe came to nursery
    Andreas, Andreas, Andreas came to nursery
Use appropriate terminology for your setting – '*Andreas came to playgroup/school today*'.

CURRICULUM GUIDANCE

Planning the visit

A positive first experience of the setting is an important step towards the following PSED* goals from the **Curriculum Guidance for the Foundation Stage** (QCA, 2000):

Feel safe and secure and demonstrate a sense of trust (yellow ss)*;

Have a sense of belonging (blue ss)*;

Have a sense of self as a member of different communities (green ss)*.

* for a list of codes used in the Curriculum Guidance sections, see page 2.

The role of the parent

The more information you can give parents about their child's visit, the better. Provide a timetable so that they know what to expect and be ready to explain each part of the timetable as the session progresses. For example, if you offer free outdoor access, explain to parents that their child can choose to go outside whenever they wish and ask parents to keep an eye on their child in the garden. Bear in mind that the routines of your setting, while obvious to you, can seem quite bewildering to a visitor.

Apart from explaining the structure of the visit, it is also useful to offer parents some pointers on how best to support their children:

- Emphasize that the aim of this visit is for the child to leave the setting with a collection of happy memories.

- Where a child wishes to stay with their parent for the entire duration of the visit, reassure the adult that this is absolutely fine. If necessary, explain to a parent that their child is in a new setting, and it is perfectly natural for them to be 'clingy'.

- Some children may not want to participate in any activity. Reassure parents that simply observing what is going on is a valuable experience in itself, and quite normal behaviour for a young child in a strange environment.

- Some children are happy to operate quite independently of their parent. If necessary, suggest to the parent that they step back and let their child explore the setting by themselves.

- Occasionally, parents find it difficult to accept that their child does not appear to want them. If this is the case, compliment them on their child's confidence and independence and remind them that it bodes well for the future.

- Let parents choose whether or not to join in snack time and group activities. If a child is happy to sit in the group by themselves, suggest that their parent sits behind them or at the side of the room. If the child wants reassurance, encourage the parent to sit inside the circle with the child on their knee.

INFORMATION LINKS

For more on:

- forming links with parents see pages 36–46.

Preparing the rest of the group

With so much care and preparation going into the preliminary visit on behalf of the new children, it is important not to forget the rest of the group. Prepare the children the day before by talking about the visit. You can then briefly remind them just before the visitors arrive. The following list covers some of the areas you may wish to discuss:

■ Explain that the visiting children may behave differently from the rest of the group. Try to handle this topic sensitively. While you need to address the possibility that the visitors will be noisier than usual, or leave their toys lying around, you do not want to set up negative expectations. Help the group to understand why the visiting children may behave differently by explaining that they are new to the setting and do not yet know the routines.

■ If necessary, explain to the group that the new children are coming in with their mummies/daddies/grandmas/childminders. If you regularly have adult helpers in the setting, this will probably not make much difference to the children. However, if additional adults are unusual in your setting, you do need to talk about why parents are accompanying their children, and that they might sit with their children during circle or snack time.

■ Ask the children to be kind and friendly to the visitors. They might need help with finding a toy or putting something away. Perhaps the children could also invite the visitors to play a game or share a book.

■ Set up a couple of role-play activities to show children some techniques for responding to the visitors. For example, greeting a visiting child and telling them your name or inviting a child to join in a game or share a book.

Observation notes

Although your main focus will be on the visiting children, it is important to observe how your established children respond to the visit.

■ How do established children cope with the disruption to their routine? Are they fazed by the change of atmosphere and noise level, or do they take it in their stride? Be ready to offer extra support to sensitive children who are unnerved by the sudden influx of strangers.

■ Observe children with special needs to see how they respond to the visit. For example, children with Asperger's syndrome may find the disruption to their routine difficult to cope with. Be ready to give extra support.

■ How do established children respond to the visitors? Are they welcoming and helpful? Do they show a tendency to take charge or even become a little 'bossy'? Evaluate your observations to decide whether you have given established children enough preparation for the visit.

■ Observing how established children cope with preliminary visits may contribute to the following points in the **Foundation Profile** assessment scales:

Social development 7

Emotional development 5 and 7

For a summary of different observational approaches, see page 4

CURRICULUM GUIDANCE

Preparing the rest of the group

Encouraging established children to consider the needs and feelings of the visiting children will help towards many PSED goals, including:

Begin to accept the needs of others, with support (yellow ss);

Consider the consequences of their words and actions for themselves and others (ELG);

Initiate interactions with other people (green ss);

Have a developing awareness of their own needs, views and feelings and be sensitive to the needs, views and feelings of others (ELG).

The first few weeks

Once new children start at your setting on a regular basis, you will need to implement the next stage of your settling-in process. Bear in mind the following:

Timetabling

The first few sessions should be shorter than usual. For example, if a full session is normally three hours, the initial session should be about 90 minutes. The following timetable provides a model for gradually increasing the length of the sessions. It can be adopted as it stands, or adapted to fit into the structure of your day:

- **Day 1**: arrive 30 minutes later than the rest of the group; session to last 90 minutes.

- **Day 2**: arrive 15 minutes later than the rest of the group; session to last two hours.

- **Day 3**: for children who are settling well, arrive at the same time as the rest of the group; session to last for 2 hours 30 minutes.

- **Day 4**: for children who are settling well, arrive and leave at the same time as the rest of the group; session to last a full three hours.

When planning the timings for your first few sessions, there are three important considerations:

- Wherever possible, arrange for new children to arrive and leave at different times from the rest of the group. The start and the end of a session are busy times, and they can be overwhelming for new children.

- Once parents start to leave their children at the setting, ask them to remain 'on call', if at all possible. Explain that it is sometimes necessary for children to be collected earlier than planned when they are first left – and that this is common and nothing to worry about.

- Be ready to adjust the timetable. Talk to each parent individually and, wherever possible, arrange arrival and departure times to suit their child's needs (see *SNAPSHOT – a flexible start*).

SNAPSHOT – a flexible start

Lauren cried incessantly once her mother started leaving her at the setting. Her key worker discussed the situation with Lauren's mother and together they devised a special timetable. They agreed that the mother would bring Lauren 30 minutes after the start of the session and stay with her while she adjusted to the setting. Once Lauren's mother had left the setting, she would remain 'on call' so that the key worker could contact her if Lauren became too distressed. They agreed that they would aim for Lauren to manage at least one hour, but the key worker reassured the mother that she would call sooner if she felt it was necessary. Gradually, Lauren adjusted to being left and by the sixth week she was happily staying by herself for the full three-hour session.

This snapshot shows the value of:

- *Responding to each child's individual needs, particularly during the settling-in period.*
- *Consultation with parents when planning an individual settling-in strategy.*
- *Giving children as much time and support as they need when adjusting to a new setting.*

Planning the first few weeks

There is no escaping the fact that the first two or three weeks will be hard going. There are always some children who need extra care and attention as they adapt to the setting, and your established children may be unsettled by the disruption to their normal routine. But, careful planning and management will get you through, the chaos will sort itself out (sometimes quite suddenly) and your setting will end up running as smoothly as ever. Hang on to that thought when you reach the middle of the second week with three distraught children, two sets of wet pants and a major juice spill, all happening at once!

TRY THIS

'My first day'

Write a simple story about the children's first day. Include all the main routines of the setting, leaving spaces to write each child's name into the story. Make a cover with the title, for example, 'Molly at *nursery/playgroup/school*'. Illustrate the story with photos and print out a copy for each child to take home. Save the story to use in future years.

Comings and goings

Two of the most important elements to get right are the 'arrivals' and the 'departures'. Plan a routine for the start and the end of the session – and follow it as closely as possible. Arriving at the setting can be an emotional flashpoint and it is reassuring for both children and parents if they know what to expect. The consistent presence of the child's key worker provides the child with a bridge between home and setting. If all key workers are waiting to receive the children and their parents as they arrive, they can welcome the children and give parents instructions. Once parents have started to leave their children in the setting, it will help both children and parents if the familiar key workers are there, waiting to take over responsibility for the children in a calm and reassuring manner.

The end of the session can also be a sensitive time, as tired and excited children are re-united with their parents. Watch the children carefully; in the excitement of being collected, trips and tumbles can often occur. When you say goodbye to the child, offer them a positive little reminder that they will be coming to the setting again: '*It was lovely to see you today, Vikram. We'll see you again tomorrow.*' Once parents have started leaving their children in the setting, 'home time' becomes a good moment to have a quick chat about how the child has settled – although it is important to give both child and parent time to greet each other properly, before engaging the adult in conversation. If there are any difficulties or serious issues to discuss, try to do so in a quiet area of the setting away from the child. Better still, arrange to have a private conversation later in the day.

CURRICULUM GUIDANCE

Comings and goings

Carefully managing the children's arrival during the early days plays an important role in the following PSED goals:

Separate from main carer with support (yellow ss);

Separate from main carer with confidence (blue ss);

Feel safe and secure and demonstrate a sense of trust (yellow ss).

Planning the session

Plan for your usual routine from day one; the sooner the children experience a normal session, the sooner they will learn what to expect. Within this structure you can then make adjustments to support the children as they adapt to the setting. For example, hold lots of small group activities during free choice time, making sure you have practitioners nearby to help children settle or remove and comfort any children who become tearful. Introduce lots of songs, action rhymes, simple activities and practical routines. Choose repetitive rhymes that encourage the children to look at, listen to and imitate the adult leading the group and repeat them on a daily basis so that the children get to know them.

Routines

During the first few weeks, the children should be introduced to the different areas and routines of the setting. The earlier you can give them 'ownership' of their surroundings, the more they will start to feel a part of their new environment. Although routines will vary from setting to setting, the following examples cover many that will be common to all:

- *Using the toilet*: asking to use the toilet; managing toilet paper; flushing the toilet…

- *Washing hands*: managing taps and soap; drying hands on a paper towel and throwing it away…

- *Going outside*: finding pegs; putting on coats and boots…

- *Outdoor safety procedures*: using climbing equipment safely; learning the difference between 'games that are fun' and 'games that hurt others'…

- *Snack and lunchtime procedures*: helping yourself to water throughout the day; managing cutlery/lunchboxes…

- *Using the book corner*: putting books back the right way round; not blocking access to the shelves when sitting down to read a book…

- *Using the writing area*: writing names on work/asking for names to be written; putting materials back where they came from…

- *Using the craft area*: putting on aprons; managing crayons, scissors and glue…

- *Setting routines*: walking indoors; respecting other children's activities; after the first few weeks, interrupting politely (see *TRY THIS – how to interrupt politely*, page 17).

During the first few weeks, keep reiterating these basic routines as often as possible. In most cases, *showing* the children what to do is more effective than telling them – try to accompany any explanation with a clear demonstration. If possible, ask established children to model routines such as interrupting politely or walking around a floor mat.

TRY THIS

How to interrupt politely

Children often need to interrupt other people when they are in the middle of something. Show them how to tap the person gently on the arm and say *'excuse me please.'* The person can then either respond immediately, or say *'I'll be with you in a minute.'* Practise the technique with role play.

INFORMATION LINKS

For more on:

- helping children to settle in groups see pages 71–82

TRY THIS

Extra help

Try to organize some extra pairs of hands for the first couple of weeks, particularly once parents have started to leave their children. Parents of established children, students and active grandparents can all be a huge support. Give clear instructions on how you wish them to help, and make sure they know practical details, such as where to find the mop. Bear in mind that helpers should not be involved in toilet procedures and will also need to be checked by the Criminal Records Bureau. Give yourself enough time to get this done.

CURRICULUM GUIDANCE

Planning the session/routines

Supporting the children in discovering what their new environment has to offer will help towards many PSED goals, including:

Show curiosity/Have a strong exploratory impulse (yellow ss);

Show increasing independence in selecting and carrying out activities (blue ss);

Display high levels of involvement in activities/Persist for extended periods of time at an activity of their choosing/Take risks and explore within the environment (green ss);

Continue to be interested, excited and motivated to learn (ELG).

Becoming familiar with the setting and establishing routines such as using the toilets will help the children feel at home. This contributes towards many PSED goals, including:

Have a sense of belonging (blue ss);

Have a sense of self as a member of different communities (green ss);

Dress and undress independently and manage their own personal hygiene (ELG).

Handling children's reactions

Many children experience some degree of separation anxiety when their parents start to leave them in the setting. Children express their anxiety in different ways, and responding to each individual reaction can be a challenge during the first few weeks. Although every child is unique, there are certain attitudes and approaches that should be adopted, regardless of the situation:

- Identify the behaviour, but never label the child. Think in terms of a 'withdrawn reaction', rather than a 'withdrawn child'.

- Always remain calm and consistent, however challenging the child's reaction, and try not to take negative behaviour personally. Remember that the child is angry/ frightened/confused about their circumstances, not about you (see *SNAPSHOT – a thick skin*, page 19).

- Always look out for the child who makes a run for the door (all staff should be aware of procedures for keeping certain doors in the setting shut).

- Be aware that for some children suffering from separation anxiety, any mention of mummy/daddy/nanny can make things worse.

INFORMATION LINKS

For more on:

- securing doors in the setting see page 54.

SNAPSHOT – a thick skin

It was the end of Taiki's first week and his mother had arrived to collect him. When she picked him up to give him a cuddle, Taiki looked at his key worker from the safety of her arms and announced: *'I don't like you – and I don't like your school!'* Taiki's mother apologized profusely, but the key worker assured her that she was not at all offended and that Taiki had really had a very good week! Two years later, they remembered the incident with some amusement when Taiki insisted on visiting the setting during half term at his new school.

This snapshot shows the value of:

- *Not taking a child's comments personally.*
- *Keeping a sense of humour and sharing happy memories with parents.*

Apart from using general approaches such as those outlined above, it can be helpful to identify the specific emotion the child is displaying and respond with some targeted strategies.

The angry reaction

Some children express their anxiety with anger. Tantrums, an 'angry' cry and aggressive actions are all hallmarks of the child who feels anger at being left in a strange new situation.

Strategies

- Acknowledge the child's anger: *'I know you feel angry because nanny isn't here – but she will come back'*. Adopt a firm tone, but make sure that your voice is also kind and comforting.

- Whatever the child does to you (hitting, kicking, punching), try to keep calm. You may need to intervene to protect yourself, but the child's physical safety should always be your first priority.

- If the child has a tantrum, you may just have to sit it out. Never, under any circumstances, leave the child alone. Sit quietly and calmly near the child, and once the tantrum is over, give lots of reassurance. Offer the opportunity to rest or engage in a quiet, calming activity.

- Extreme reactions can be frightening for other children – and tears can be contagious. In this instance, you should put the needs of the group first and take the child out of the setting. However, this should be a last resort. It will not help the child to adjust to the setting if their anger results in them regularly being taken elsewhere.

■ Try distraction. Sometimes, an appealing toy or the involvement of a friendly (and robust) established child can help the child forget their anger and engage in something more positive (see *SNAPSHOT – distraction techniques*).

■ Take time out for yourself. Although it is preferable for new children to form a primary relationship with just one adult in the setting, anger can be exhausting to deal with. Ask colleagues for support and help in sharing the load.

SNAPSHOT – distraction techniques

Hayley reacted with anger at being left by her mother. After attempting to calm her screams (and protect herself from being kicked) the key worker took Hayley into a side-room. She tried to distract her with different toys, books and rhymes, but nothing worked. She then hit upon the idea of telling Hayley about her own daughter, who happened to have the same name: *'I've got a big girl called Hayley,'* she told the child. Hayley immediately stopped crying, looked crossly at the key worker and said: *'I don't like that Hayley!'* In spite of her words, Hayley was intrigued. She forgot her tears and listened intently to an impromptu story about 'big Hayley'. When the key worker took her back into the setting, two older children came up and invited a much calmer Hayley to help them with a puzzle, giving the key worker a welcome break.

This snapshot shows the value of:

■ *Persisting until you find a way of getting through to a child.*

■ *Using distraction techniques, particularly when the activity or conversational topic has some personal meaning to the child.*

■ *The role of established children in helping new ones to settle.*

The fearful reaction

The fearful, anxious reaction can often be easier to handle than the angry reaction. However, anxiety and shyness can last for a very long time, with the child showing reluctance to try new activities or strike out on their own.

Strategies

■ Give the fearful child plenty of attention. Keep them with you at all times – let them sit beside you during group activities and be ready to support them at times of transition, such as going outside.

- Gaining the trust of anxious children is a vital step towards helping them settle. In the early weeks, the child's key worker should be a consistent and reliable presence in the setting.

- Remember that the child will eventually have to be weaned off their reliance on one particular adult in the setting. Follow your instincts as to the right moment, and make sure the process is carried out slowly and gently. For example, suggest that another practitioner helps with putting on boots; invite the child to sit one seat away from you, next to a sympathetic established child. Eventually, the child *will* follow one of these suggestions and the detachment process can begin.

- However tempting, never try to 'hoodwink' the fearful child in an attempt to make a situation seem less scary (see *SNAPSHOT – nanny in the garden*). For example, if a child is anxious about being collected, give a simple, honest response: *'Daddy has gone shopping – he will come back later to collect you'*. At the same time, soften the message with reassurance: *'He won't forget to come back for his special boy – let's have a good time so we can tell him all about it when he comes to get you.'*

- Developing friendships is often the best way for the fearful child to settle. Help the child to join in with other children – and keep on trying if the child is unwilling to participate (see *SNAPSHOT – joining in*, pages 113–114).

- If you and the child's parents feel that their presence will help the child to settle, accommodate the parents staying with their child for as long as necessary (see *SNAPSHOT – a flexible start*, page 14, for an example of a mother withdrawing gradually).

SNAPSHOT – nanny in the garden

Staff had observed that outdoor play was causing Sean some anxiety during his first few days in the setting. He spent most of his time in the garden looking behind bushes and peering into the play house, as if searching for something. Once back indoors, he would be particularly upset and tearful. His key worker talked to him and discovered that he thought his nanny was hiding in the garden. When Sean's nanny came to collect him, the key worker mentioned her concerns and the nanny admitted that she had tried to calm Sean's separation anxiety by telling him that she would stay in the garden. The key worker tactfully suggested a different approach. Together they agreed to give Sean the same clear message that the nanny would go shopping while Sean was at nursery, emphasizing that she would be there to collect him after going home group. Sean's anxiety gradually lessened and he started to relax and enjoy outdoor activities.

This snapshot shows the value of:

- *Looking beneath the surface of a child's reaction to find the true cause of their distress.*
- *Consulting with parents or carers to find clues as to why a child is distressed.*
- *Giving children clear, honest explanations pitched at their level of understanding.*

TRY THIS

Welcome bags

Give each new child a drawstring bag and ask parents to help their child put a few items from home inside their bag. For example:

- a small comfort toy
- photographs of family members
- a favourite book
- a small belonging that parents are happy to lend the child.

Use the bag as a talking point and a link with home. Help children to integrate by inviting them to show their special items to others.

TRY THIS

Using picture books

Martin Waddell's *Owl Babies* (Walker Books) is a charming and reassuring picture book to share with any child who has ever worried about being left alone.

The withdrawn reaction

Some children are unwilling to engage with adults or other children, or participate in any activities. In a busy setting, such children can easily be overlooked as they are not 'troublesome'. However, they need as much support as children who react in a more obvious or voluble manner.

Strategies

- Keep on trying to include the withdrawn child. Treat them as though they are fully integrated; for example, always offer them their turn during games, even if you suspect they won't respond. In the vast majority of cases, they *will* join in eventually.

- Never draw attention to a child's lack of involvement (see *SNAPSHOT – an inappropriate response*, page 23). Simply greet each mute response with a warm, friendly smile and always keep alive the possibility of participating in the future – '*you can have a turn next time, Assia*'.

- Respect the child who wants to observe before participating in an activity. Observation is a vital means of learning and many young children cope with a new situation by watching what is happening, before joining in.

■ Drawing a child out of their shell can seem to take forever. As long as you are offering appropriate support procedures, have faith that the vast majority will settle and participate in the end.

A persistent and excessively withdrawn, anxious or angry reaction may indicate that a child has special needs lasting beyond the normal settling-in period. Observe the child closely, consult with parents and follow the procedures in your Special Needs policy. Prepare and implement an Individual Education Plan (IEP) if necessary.

INFORMATION LINKS

For information on:

■ writing and implementing a Special Needs policy

■ writing and implementing IEPs

■ supporting children with special needs: see Further Reading.

SNAPSHOT – an inappropriate response

Although Joseph was willing to sit in a group with other children, he would not communicate with anyone in the setting or participate in the activity. A student was conducting a small group activity, asking the children to name different animals in a picture book. When it came to Joseph's turn, he whispered the name of an animal. The student immediately responded with the comment: *'Joseph, you've decided to talk to me at last'*. Fortunately, the child's key worker was assisting with the group. At the end of the activity, she emphasized the importance of not drawing attention to Joseph's silence. She then observed Joseph carefully, ready to encourage any further communication and offer extra support if needed.

This snapshot shows the value of:

■ *Responding positively to children at all times and taking care never to draw negative attention to a child's difficulties.*

■ *Ensuring that all adults (including students and helpers) know of any special approaches to individual children or IEPs.*

■ *Observing children following a sensitive incident, to check how they have been affected.*

The delayed reaction

A delayed reaction to starting in the setting is a surprisingly common event. Typically, a child settles quite happily and then seems to realize, about two weeks later, that 'this is for real'.

Strategies

■ Be prepared for the delayed reaction. Remember that it is quite normal and that the child will settle again in the end.

■ The delayed reaction can take many different forms. Use whichever strategies seem appropriate, just as you would have done had the child reacted with anger, anxiety or withdrawal during the first few days.

■ If parents are concerned about a delayed reaction, reassure them that it is a common phenomenon and that it will pass.

INFORMATION LINKS

For more on:

■ anger and other behavioural challenges see pages 111–22.

■ supporting parents during the first few weeks see pages 42–3.

Observation notes

Observe new children closely during the first few weeks to help you establish how they are settling.

■ Observe children as they arrive in the setting. How easily do they separate from their parents? How quickly do they settle once they are left? If parents are staying, keep an eye on whether the child is starting to engage independently with activities and interact with other children and adults as the session progresses.

■ Watch out for any children who are having particular difficulty settling, and use your observations as the basis for putting in extra support. Liaise with parents and plan a settling-in programme to meet the child's needs (for an example see *SNAPSHOT – a flexible start*, page 14).

■ Look out for a 'delayed reaction' amongst those children who settle well initially (see *The delayed reaction*, above).

■ Your initial observations should focus on how the children are settling. Once they have started to adjust to their new surroundings, look out for how they function within the setting, for example:

- their level of physical development;
- their level of language development;
- how well they respond to verbal instructions;
- how they interact with other children and adults in the setting;
- how quickly they are able to absorb routines;
- how they cope with changes in routines;
- how well they engage with activities;
- what particular activities they are attracted to;
- how well they settle and participate in group activities.

Use these observations as the basis for your planning. For example, some children might need lots of support with physical development activities; you may have children who show a talent for painting and need to be stretched; if children are struggling to manage their coats, keep showing them a simple technique and give them lots of chance to practise.

■ Look out for children with delayed speech or physical development, children who have difficulty interacting with adults and other children and any other indication that may suggest special needs. Observe a child closely to gather as much information as possible and follow the procedures set out in your Special Needs policy.

■ Observing children during the first few weeks may contribute to the following points in the **Foundation Profile** assessment scales:

■ how children settle:

- *Emotional development 1* and *2*

■ how children participate in groups and individual activities:

- *Disposition and attitudes 1* and *3*
- *Social development 3* and *4*.

■ For examples of observation in practice, see Snapshots on pages 21 and 23.

For a summary of different observational approaches, see page 4.

CURRICULUM GUIDANCE

Handling different reactions

How you manage a child's separation anxiety plays an important part in the following PSED goals:

Separate from main carer with support (yellow ss);

Separate from main carer with confidence (blue ss);

Feel safe and secure and demonstrate a sense of trust (yellow ss);

Relate and make attachments to members of their group (yellow ss).

Making links between home and the setting with activities such as a 'welcome bag' (see page 22) can help towards the following PSED goals:

Talk freely about their home and community (blue ss);

Have a sense of self as a member of different communities (green ss).

Parent partnerships

From the moment a child first arrives in your setting, you are entering into an important relationship with that child's parents. The exchange of information about the child and the setting, the support you give the parents and the support the parents give you will all contribute to a positive partnership.

The chapter is divided into three sections:

■ Exchanging information

■ Parent meetings

■ Supporting parents.

Exchanging information

Although the exchange of information will continue throughout a child's time with you, it is particularly important to keep parents well informed while they are getting to know the setting.

The following framework provides you with ample opportunity to give parents all the information they need:

■ send a prospectus in response to initial enquiries

■ invite parents for an introductory visit

■ invite the child to visit, accompanied by their parents

■ fill out an enrolment form

■ provide a copy of the Policies and Procedures for your setting.

INFORMATION LINKS

For more on:

■ Policies and Procedures see pages 31—4 and Further Reading.

The prospectus

For many parents, the prospectus offers a first taste of the setting. While it is important that a prospectus should reflect the unique character of your setting, there is certain information that should be included in any prospectus. The following format can be used as a framework for developing or updating your own prospectus.

- ■ **Introductory letter**:
  - express appreciation of the parents' interest in the setting
  - emphasize your high levels of commitment to the children's care
  - invite parents and children to visit the setting.

- ■ **Philosophy and aims**: for example –
  - to provide a secure, happy environment
  - to facilitate a smooth transition from home to setting
  - to develop in the children a love and respect for themselves, others and the environment
  - to awaken curiosity and interest
  - to encourage the development of independence, confidence and self control
  - to provide experiences suited to the developmental needs of all children
  - to make appropriate provision for children with special needs
  - to develop communication skills
  - to develop physical co-ordination skills
  - to prepare children for transition to Reception.

- ■ **Location**: the address of the setting, plus a map showing the location.

- ■ **The physical setting**: a description of the premises, including the different areas of the setting (cloakrooms, dining area, rest area, writing, craft and book areas, different play settings, outdoor play areas).

- **Equipment**: a list showing your range of equipment. For example –

  - a large collection of picture books, including poetry, story and information books reflecting different races, languages, cultures and family groupings

  - a wide range of musical instruments

  - materials for cutting, sticking, drawing, painting, modelling and writing

  - resources to encourage imaginative play, including dressing-up clothes, puppets and small world play

  - resources for science and technology, including programmable toys and computers

  - a wide variety of construction toys, such as Duplo and Polydrons

  - living things to care for

  - equipment for gardening, cooking and water activities

  - indoor and outdoor sandpits, climbing frames and soft play equipment

  - tricycles and other outdoor toys.

- **The Areas of Learning**: a brief explanation of how you help the children's development within the six Areas of Learning, both indoors and outdoors.

- **Sessions**: session times, approximate term times, arrival/departure times, plus details of extra provision, such as 'early starts', after school care and holiday care.

- **Fees**: if relevant to your setting:

  - a separate leaflet detailing fees and up-to-date information about Government funding for three and four year olds

  - further information about fees, including when payable, late payment charges, additional fees for extra activities, fees payable in lieu of a term's notice if child is withdrawn.

- **Admissions procedure**: information about waiting lists, introductory visits, enrolment (including a copy of your enrolment form) and settling-in procedures.

- **Equal Opportunities policy**: outline your Equal Opportunities policy, for example –

  Staff have a policy of treating all children equally, without regard to their sex, race, religion, colour, creed, ethnic or national origin or any disability they may have. This policy is reflected in any interactions between the setting and the child's parents and carers. We also adhere to this policy when recruiting, employing and training all staff within the setting.

- **Special Needs policy**: outline your policy for children with special needs. For example –

> *Children with special needs are welcomed in our setting. Our Special Education Needs Co-ordinator (SENCO) will take responsibility for developing and implementing an Individual Education Plan (IEP) for any child with special needs, in full consultation with the child's parents. Wherever necessary, we draw upon outside advice and support. If we feel that a child has a special educational need after they have been admitted to the setting, we will communicate our observations in writing. In liaising with external experts and putting an IEP in place, the needs of the child will always be put first. Our SENCO will also be responsible for arranging regular staff training in special needs provision.*

- **Health and Safety**: outline your Health and Safety policy, including:

  – compliance with local child protection procedures

  – procedures for emergency medical treatment/the Accident book

  – procedures for regular fire drills/checking fire equipment

  – procedures for checking staff/adult visitors

  – procedures for the supervision of children

  – procedures for ensuring safety in the physical environment, including doors, windows, garden, play equipment, storage of equipment, gas/electrical equipment

  – food/kitchen hygiene

  – toilet/nappy changing hygiene

  – animals in the setting

  – safety procedures for outings

  – details of insurance cover and staff training in health and safety.

- **Behaviour policy**: outline your Behaviour policy (see pages 132–3).

- **Complaints policy**: outline your Complaints policy (see page 45).

The exploratory visit

The exploratory visit enables parents to observe the setting in operation, get a feel for the atmosphere and have a look at the physical environment, equipment and activities on offer. If it is your first meeting with the parents, it is also the start of a very important relationship, so it does need to be carefully planned and managed.

Double-check that parents have received a prospectus before their visit and invite them to arrive about 30 minutes after the start of a session. This gives both children and staff a chance to settle, as well as making it easier for you to plan a free period of time. Although every parent will have different areas of interest, aim to cover the following:

- Explain the structure of a session.

- Point out the balance between adult- and child-initiated activities (explain the difference, if necessary).

- Show parents around the setting.

- Point out different events in the setting to illustrate some of your aims and philosophy; for example, a child clearing up independently after painting or a group planting seeds in the garden.

- Make it clear to parents that they are only getting a quick 'snapshot' of the setting during an initial short visit.

Give parents ample time for any questions raised by the visit or the prospectus. Withdrawing to a separate space with the offer of refreshments can help parents relax and engage in a positive conversation. Explain your admissions procedures so that they can enrol their child, should they decide that the setting is for them. Always remember to ask them to sign the visitors' book when they arrive.

TRY THIS

Just parents!

Suggest to parents that they make an initial visit to the setting without their child. They often find it easier to observe what is happening and ask questions if they do not have to focus on their child at the same time. Encourage parents to bring their child on a separate visit and explain that their child will be offered a programme of preliminary visits, prior to starting in the setting.

Policies, procedures and 'official' information

Once parents have decided to enrol their child in your setting, you will need to give them a comprehensive 'Policies and Procedures' document. They, in their turn, should give you information about themselves and their child. The following list can be used as a framework for the areas you need to cover:

- **Communication**: most parents appreciate being given specific times when staff will be available to discuss any concerns. For your own sake, set some limits – for example, between 4.00 and 5.00 pm on weekdays. If you are also able to offer a time slot in the evening, this will be useful for working parents who might find it difficult to contact you during the day. Give parents the setting's telephone numbers, e-mail and website addresses. Emphasize the parents' responsibility to keep you informed of any change in their contact details and provide you with details of an alternative adult to contact in an emergency.

■ **Delivering/releasing children**: let parents know that it is their responsibility to inform both the setting and the child if anyone other than the usual carer collects the child. Explain procedures for late arrival and request that parents are as punctual as possible. Apart from helping the setting to run more smoothly, explain how distressed many children become if they are left waiting. If relevant, give details of additional charges that will be levied for parents who are late in collecting their children.

■ **Possessions from home**: ask parents to name items brought in from home (boots, coats, jumpers, water bottles, books). List the kinds of items you welcome from home, such as exhibits for the nature table or a special book to share with the group. Request that items are taken home and clarify that the setting cannot take responsibility for any item that is left at the end of the day.

■ **Snacks and lunchtimes**: outline snack and lunchtime procedures for prepared lunches and/or packed lunches:

 – *Prepared lunches*: ask parents to inform you of food allergies and intolerances; give sample menus and a brief description of lunchtime procedures (children helping to set tables, learning to use cutlery); give prices and payment details.

 – *Packed lunches*: suggest suitable foods and a list of foods you would prefer children not to bring.

■ **Policies and procedures for**:

 – Equal Opportunities

 – Special Needs

 – Behaviour

 – Health and Safety

 – Complaints.

 Although it is advisable to cover these areas in your prospectus, they should also be fully described in your 'Policies and Procedures' documentation. When writing these sections, bear in mind that a *policy* means '*what the setting plans to do*', while a *procedure* means '*how the setting intends to implement the policy*'. For example, treating all children equally is a policy, whereas providing a range of picture books representing disability, different family groupings and a variety of cultural backgrounds is a procedure for achieving this policy.

■ **Clothing, footwear and sun protection**: include a list of what you require parents to provide, for example:

  – clothes that are easy to take on and off with minimum adult help; avoid tightly buckled belts, braces or difficult buttons (track suits are easy and practical)

  – sleeves that are short enough to be rolled up easily, to avoid wet cuffs during water activities

  – everyday clothing that will not inhibit children from joining in 'messy play'

  – named Wellington boots

  – named indoor shoes that are easy to put on, for example, slip-ons or Velcro straps; avoid laces and stiff buckles

  – a spare change of clothes (in a named bag)

  – sun cream and a brimmed sun hat during summer (in a named bag).

■ **Illness/allergies**: emphasize parents' responsibility to tell you about any medical conditions or allergies. Explain procedures for informing the setting if a child is ill and, if possible, provide an e-mail address and/or telephone answering machine for working parents who may only be able to contact you early in the morning. Inform parents of the setting's responsibility to protect all children from the unnecessary risk of infection and ask them to keep their child at home in the event of:

  – a temperature

  – sickness and/or diarrhoea during the night

  – heavy cold/cough

  – any other obviously infectious illness or signs of being too unwell to cope with nursery.

Ask parent to inform you if their child has an infectious illness such as chickenpox, or needs treatment for head lice.

■ **Medication/first aid**: request that parents provide a signed letter giving permission for medicine to be administered. Medication must be labelled with clear written instructions and given directly to a staff member. It should never be put in the child's lunchbox or bag. Parents will also be requested to fill in and sign the Medication book with the dosage/times of dosage. The Medication book will then be signed by a staff member when the medication is administered and countersigned by another staff member. Outline your first aid kit and training.

■ **Consent**: inform parents that they will need to give consent for events such as outings and photographs, without which the child cannot participate.

- **Records**: explain what information will be kept about a child, how it is gathered, where it is kept and who has access.

- **Parents' meetings**: outline how parents will be kept informed of their child's progress; describe your typical programme of parents' evenings, information sessions and parent groups.

- **Parent helpers**: explain how parents can support the setting – for example, helping with cooking or musical activities; getting involved with fundraising/parents' groups.

- **Staff**: describe your staff and management structure, including the 'key worker' system.

Bear in mind that you may need to make this information accessible to parents in a variety of different ways; for example, in Braille, in different languages, as an audio tape or through an interpreter.

INFORMATION LINKS

For more on:

- keeping records see pages 3–5.

- parents' meetings see pages 36–42.

TRY THIS

Repeating information

Aim to deliver an important piece of information in at least three different ways. For example, for a forthcoming trip:

1 send a letter home
2 put up an eye-catching notice on your notice board
3 ask staff to mention the trip to parents when they collect their children.

'Informal' information

The previous section covers the exchange of 'official' and written information. There is, however, a whole host of informal information that can be just as important in building good parent partnerships and helping children to settle. While chatting with parents and children, keep an ear out for details such as:

- preferred nicknames (although beware adopting a family nickname without the child's consent)

- names for family members (the child who is looked after by 'Nan' will be very confused if you refer to her as 'Granny')

- interests, likes, dislikes and fears

- family structure/sibling relationships

- when the child started to walk/talk

- any difficulties with birth

- significant family events that may affect the child

- any snippets of information that could suggest special needs (treat such information as just one clue and keep it in perspective).

It is important that this information gathering does not turn into an invasion of privacy. In the process of forming a relationship with parents, simply be aware of anything that crops up (and treat such information as confidential).

TRY THIS

Child's record

Ask parents and child to fill in a record sheet together. Include questions such as the child's preferred name, the names of siblings, pets, favourite activities and foods. Although the adult will be writing in the answers, have space for the child to add their own mark making. The record can be filled in at home, or used as a shared activity for parent, key worker and child during the first few days in the setting.

TRY THIS

A website

A website can be a useful way of disseminating information. Include anything from the dates of parents' evenings to advice on lunchboxes and outdoor clothing. Ask around for any parents who might be willing to help you with the website.

Parent meetings

Parent meetings can range from discussions about an individual child's progress to information sessions and social gatherings.

Meetings for new parents

Although you will be having daily contact with parents or carers when the children are collected, it is reassuring for parents to have a planned meeting fairly soon after their child has started in the setting. Four to six weeks gives most children (and parents) long enough to go through the normal settling-in process. How you organize the meeting will depend on each individual setting. The following format can be adopted as it stands or adapted to fit in with your particular way of working:

- Staff members greet parents and offer refreshments.

- A short, informal talk to the parents as a group. This is an opportunity to reiterate certain policies and procedures, for example:

  - the philosophy and aims of the setting

  - the routines of the day

  - a run through practical details, such as wearing appropriate clothing.

  If parents are being a bit forgetful about routines, take the opportunity to give reminders (but avoid making them feel 'ticked off').

- A question-and-answer session.

- An opportunity for parents to talk individually with staff about how their child has settled in.

TRY THIS

Anonymous questions

A question-and-answer session can be the most useful part of any talk. Encourage reticent parents to ask questions with an anonymous question box. Have a short refreshment break after the talk, provide parents with pencils and paper and ask them to write out their questions to put in the box. Give yourself time to read through the questions first – this enables you to deal with similar questions in one go and have a quick think about anything tricky.

Suggestions for parents' talks

Talks and discussion groups are a useful means of giving parents background information about their child's learning and development. You may need to mention that this is not a time for discussing individual children (if necessary, remind parents of how to contact you for an individual meeting). The talks can cover just about any topic:

- **Becoming a communicator**: how communication skills help children develop socially and as learners.

- **Literacy**: the importance of conversation, nursery rhymes, songs and picture books; the development of reading and writing skills.

- **Creativity and the imagination**: including art, craft, design and construction, music, singing, dance, dressing up and role play.

- **Unfamiliar activities**: an introduction to activities that may be new to parents, such as 'messy' or 'small world' play.

- **Curriculum Guidance for the Foundation stage**: an explanation of the six Areas of Learning, the Stepping Stones and Early Learning Goals.

- **Curriculum areas**: focusing on single areas of learning, such as Mathematical development or Physical development.

- **Record keeping**: an explanation of how you make observations, what you look out for and the Foundation Stage Profile.

- **Learning outdoors**: how you maximize the children's access to the garden and what they can learn from the outdoor environment.

- **Encouraging positive behaviour**: how you deal with different behavioural challenges and encourage positive behaviour, with reference to your Behaviour policy.

- **Parenting issues**: helping parents with behavioural challenges at home, for example –

  - mealtimes/fussy eaters

  - bedtime routines

  - toilet training

  - sibling relationships

  - tantrums/confrontations

  - rudeness/bad language

  - separation anxiety

  - the sensitive child.

■ **Transition to Reception**: information on helping children transfer to the next stage of their education.

INFORMATION LINKS

For more on:

■ record keeping see pages 3–5.

■ learning outdoors see pages 102–8.

■ encouraging positive behaviour see pages 132–3.

When planning your talk, you need to ask yourself the following questions:

■ **Is the topic relevant and of interest to this particular group of parents?**
Find out by chatting to parents and asking them what they want (see *TRY THIS – what do parents want?*, page 40)

■ **Is the session pitched at an appropriate level?**
Some parents like to cover a topic in depth, others prefer a more practical approach with the chance to try out activities and chat informally to staff. Inviting parents to fill out an evaluation sheet will give you some idea of whether your approach was appropriate.

■ **Is the session varied and interesting?**
Are you using several different ways to present the information – for example, visual aids, a slide show, 'hands-on' activities and a question and answer session? Remember that most people cannot take in much more than a 30-minute talk, particularly in the evening!

■ **Do you have sufficient expertise?**
If you do not feel confident about a topic, invite an outside speaker to join you. For example, your local health visitor may be willing to help you with a group dicussing parenting challenges.

■ **Have you prepared a handout?**
Many parents like to take away a handout. Include simple suggestions of activities parents can do at home with their children and a summary of the topic. Keep a sample so that you can reproduce copies for future talks.

SNAPSHOT – a literacy evening

A group of parents had expressed an interest in finding out more about literacy development. In response to this interest, staff planned an evening with the following aims:

- to define the meaning of 'literacy development';
- to show the range of activities and experiences that contribute to literacy development;
- to demonstrate that play is an important means of learning.

Several different resources were selected, including:

- the dolls house;
- a nursery rhyme anthology, alphabet book and story book;
- percussion instruments;
- an alphabet puzzle;
- blackboards/white boards;
- paper/labels/envelopes;
- various writing implements;
- the post office role play area with letter box and postperson's outfit;
- a letter sorting activity;
- a lotto game matching simple words and pictures.

Each resource was displayed alongside a written explanation of how it contributes to literacy development.

The evening began with a short introduction to literacy. Parents were then invited to explore the resources, with staff available to answer questions. At the end of the evening, parents were given a handout summarizing literacy development and suggesting picture books, nursery rhymes and games to share with their children.

This snapshot shows the value of:

- *Finding out what parents want from a parents' evening and planning accordingly.*
- *Offering a balance of background information, 'hands on' experiences and the opportunity to ask questions.*
- *Giving parents written information to take away with them.*

Individual parents' meetings

Individual meetings are a chance to share information with the child's parents and discuss any concerns. Remember that the meeting should be a two-way dialogue, and every bit as important a source of information for you as for the parents.

The first step is to decide on dates and times. Meetings held during the autumn enable you to address any matters that come up at the start of the year. Meetings held during the summer enable you to demonstrate how children have progressed throughout the year. If possible, spread the meetings across a week or two so that you can spend plenty

TRY THIS

What do parents want?

Put up a notice explaining that you are planning parent information evenings for the coming year. Give a list of possible topics and ask parents to tick the topics that most interest them. Include space for parents to write up their own suggestions. As you chat informally to parents, listen out for topics they might be interested in.

TRY THIS

Children showing their parents around the setting

Set aside a morning or afternoon for your older children (4+) to show their parents around the setting. Explain to the children that when their mummies/daddies/grandparents visit, they can show them all the things they like to do. Send parents a letter covering the following points:

■ **The structure of the visit**: times, dates, how long it will last and whether parents can take their child home with them afterwards.

■ **The purpose of the visit**: explain that the visit is an opportunity for children to play host to their parents and choose for themselves what they want to show their parents.

■ **What parents will gain**: explain that the visit will show parents a huge amount about the setting from their child's point of view, including their child's talents, interests, likes, dislikes and how they spend their time.

■ **Parents' role: ask** parents to let their child take the lead in choosing what to show them.

■ **Staff involvement**: explain that staff will take a back seat, only involving themselves where absolutely necessary. Ask parents to contact staff later in the day if they wish to discuss anything arising from the visit.

of time with each parent. If you are just having one or two meetings a year, plan for a good 30 minutes. A well-managed meeting is time-consuming and parents should not be made to feel rushed, particularly if there are sensitive issues to discuss. Try to accommodate working parents by offering both afternoon and evening appointments.

Many parents approach parents' meetings with anxiety, particularly if they do not feel comfortable in an educational environment. As you work at helping parents to relax, bear in mind the following:

■ Be aware of your body language. Make eye contact, smile and adopt a relaxed manner (practise with colleagues if you are not confident about this).

- Parenting is a tough job – and unlike that of the early years practitioner, it doesn't end at 5.00 pm! Be sympathetic towards the pressures of parenting, find positive things to say about every child and remember to thank parents for the support they give the setting.

- Although you should aim to present yourself as a competent professional, try to avoid coming across as 'the expert'. Never make parents feel judged – in the face of any problems, they will be much more responsive to your suggestions if they perceive you as understanding and sympathetic.

- Always ask parents how they feel their child is getting on. Make it clear that they know their children better than anyone and that you value what they have to say. Listen carefully to anything that parents choose to tell you about themselves, their family life and their attitude towards their child. This kind of information can further your understanding of a child's behaviour, as well as making it easier for you to respond sensitively to any difficulties they may be having.

- Remember that the process of building a positive relationship with parents begins from the moment they first visit the setting. Have friendly little chats whenever you see them, and share positive anecdotes about their child. Establishing a friendly informal relationship will give you a great head start when it comes to putting them at their ease during a parents' evening.

Having done everything you can to establish a relaxed, positive atmosphere, you need to move on to the child's progress and development. Preparation is key to a successful meeting. Make sure that you are in a private space and check that you have all necessary information to hand. This may include:

- Records of plans showing what the child has done/will be doing as the year progresses.

- Copies of individual records and observations, including the Foundation Stage Profile.

- Samples of the child's drawing, mark making, writing and other 'work'.

- Records supporting any issues you need to raise, such as the register if you wish to discuss attendance.

One way to launch the discussion is to write a short report, either to crib from or read directly to the parents. This will help to make sure you cover everything. A written report is also useful in giving you something to focus on if you don't know the parents well or have some delicate issues to raise. Give parents a copy of the report if they ask for it.

If you do have anything negative to say, check that you have sound evidence. Make a specific statement and avoid generalizations and dramatic language – for example, *'We have noticed that Christopher has difficulty playing with other children'* rather than *'We are very worried about Christopher's violent behaviour'*. Some examples of Christopher's behaviour will also help to paint a picture of the situation. Having raised your concerns, move swiftly on to discussing possible strategies. This will help to reassure parents that the problem is being addressed, and that their input is valued. However concerned you are about a child, be as positive as possible and emphasize that most children grow out of these phases.

TRY THIS

The 'sandwich' approach

If you have to raise an area of concern, try sandwiching it between two positive statements. For example:

■ begin by talking about the child's excellent concentration

■ move on to discussing the anxiety the child displays about going outside

■ finish off by talking about the child's positive friendships with other children.

Supporting parents

Addressing problems in a positive and supportive manner is essential to good parent partnerships. Whether parents are anxious, angry or making a specific complaint, the way you respond can make a big difference to how they feel about you and the setting. Although each set of circumstances is unique, there are certain parental responses that you will have to deal with from time to time.

The first few weeks

Some parents need almost as much support as their children during the first few weeks. Many react to separating from their child with anxiety and tears – just like the children. If you end up feeling as much of a counsellor as an early years worker, remind yourself that in calming the parent, you will also be helping to calm the child.

Strategies

■ Always try to present yourself as friendly, pleasant and reliable. You are in *loco parentis*, and parents need to feel that you are trustworthy.

■ However frustrated you might feel during the early weeks, avoid passing on any negative feelings about a childs' difficulties in settling.

■ Develop a mindset that the child will settle in the end, and pass this on to the parents. It is very reassuring for the parent to be told that their child's reaction falls within normal parameters – as the vast majority do.

■ Draw on your experience. For example, although delayed separation anxiety is new and confusing to many parents, reassure them that it is very common, you have seen it numerous times before and that it will pass.

■ Keep parents informed. If extra support is needed, discuss strategies and agree on a special plan to help the child settle (see *SNAPSHOT – a flexible start*, page 14).

Anxiety

Although it is normal for parents to worry from time to time, some parents do not find it easy to let go of their anxiety.

Strategies

■ Be patient and give as much support as possible. Always remember that a parent's anxieties are very real to them, even if the source of their anxiety does not seem particularly significant to you as an experienced professional.

■ Listen to the parent's concerns and take them seriously. Could the setting be doing more to address whatever is worrying the parent? Reassure parents that you will observe their child closely, respond to the situation and keep them informed as to their child's progress.

■ Always give calming reassurance, even if you have real concerns about the child. Try to avoid taking on the parent's anxiety and aim to keep things in perspective.

■ Accept that you may have to respond to all a parent's concerns, particularly in the early days. At the same time, do consider setting some limits. If dropping-off time is not a good moment to address a long list of worries, arrange an appointment later in the day so that you can have a proper chat.

■ Be sensitive to the fact that a parent's general anxiety may be increased by difficulties in their personal or working life. You don't have to become overly involved, but it can be easier to sympathize once you discover the pressures a parent is under.

■ Suggest to the parent that they should try not to pass their anxiety onto the child – although you do have to be sensitive over this one! If you suspect that a parent might end up feeling even more anxious by such a suggestion, leave well alone.

Anger

Anger can come from many different sources. Personality, home pressures and a learned response can all result in an angry reaction to a perceived problem. The angry parent can be intimidating to deal with. Even if you feel the anger is misplaced, it is useful to have some strategies up your sleeve to help you respond quickly and effectively.

Strategies

■ If an angry parent approaches you at a busy moment, try to arrange an appointment so that you can discuss their concerns in private. Give recognition to their feelings with a clear statement such as: *'I understand that you are very angry'*. At the same time, make it clear that you are not arranging an appointment to fob them off, but in order to give them your full attention: *'It's important that we try and sort out your concerns. Can we meet later today so we can have a proper talk?'*

■ Parental anger often stems from the feeling that they are not being taken seriously. Always try to respond to anger with calmness, sympathy and understanding. In many cases, this will be enough to diffuse the anger, so that you can get on with addressing the problem.

■ Sometimes it's hard not to meet anger with anger, particularly if you feel you are being unfairly accused. Work at maintaining a professional detachment and try not to take a parent's anger personally.

■ Once you have given a parent time to express their anger, try to establish the nature of their concerns. Discuss how you might address the problem and follow the procedure set out in your Complaints policy (see *Handling complaints*, below).

■ Even if you disagree with the parent, you should still outline all you are doing to support and nurture their child. Reassure them that you will pay special attention to whatever is causing their anger.

■ If you have the slightest concern over your physical safety, make sure that you have another staff member with you. Arrange to meet the parent away from the other children.

Handling complaints

Complaints can range from worries over a child's progress to serious issues such as bullying or neglect. Following an established Complaints policy will help you to deal with complaints in a positive and supportive manner.

Strategies

■ Always try to resolve a complaint informally. Discuss strategies, ask parents for their input and reassure them that you will give their child extra time and attention (see *SNAPSHOT – a complaint about garden play*, page 45).

■ Keep parents informed of progress. Arrange a follow-up telephone call and/or meetings. This will go a long way towards helping parents feel that their complaint is being addressed.

■ Where relevant, ensure that parents understand the seriousness of their complaint. For example, in the case of possible abuse, explain that such a complaint could become a child protection issue. The purpose of this is not in any way to dissuade parents from making a valid complaint, but to let them know the full potential outcome of their allegations.

■ If you suspect that a complaint might become serious or protracted, make sure that you have another member of staff present during all meetings.

■ If you are unable to solve a problem informally, a Complaints policy gives both you and the parent a structure to follow. Check that your policy is in place and up-to-date, for example:

– Parents who are concerned about any aspect of the setting's provision should first discuss their worries with the child's key worker and/or setting manager.

– If an initial discussion does not resolve the situation or the problems persist, parents should put their concerns in writing.

– If the problem cannot be resolved through informal discussion, parents should request a formal meeting with the setting manager and other relevant individuals (such as the setting owner or chair of management committee).

– If this meeting does not lead to agreement, an external mediator (such as staff from the Pre-school Learning Alliance) will be asked to help review the situation, suggest further strategies and monitor progress.

– Written records of meetings will be agreed and signed by all present.

– At any stage of the process, parents may contact OFSTED (include address/telephone number of OFSTED regional centre).

– All complaints will be logged in the setting's Complaints book.

SNAPSHOT – a complaint about garden play

Three mothers made a complaint about aggressive behaviour in the garden and how it was affecting their children. During an informal discussion, the setting manager established the mothers' concern that this behaviour went unnoticed by staff. When asked how they wished to see the problem addressed, they expressed the view that staff should offer closer supervision and more organized play. The manager explained her reasons for having free play time in the garden, including:

■ the opportunity for children to plan their own games in a more spacious environment

■ the opportunity to use a range of motor skills such as running and jumping

■ the opportunity to explore a natural environment independently.

She reassured the parents that staff would monitor the children's behaviour closely and discuss garden play. Following a meeting with all staff, the following strategies were agreed:

■ where necessary, staff should intervene in group games to offer a more positive focus

■ all staff should make extra efforts to implement appropriate and firm behavioural boundaries in the outdoor setting, just as they do in the indoor setting

■ group discussions should be held to help children understand the difference between games that are fun and games that hurt others

SNAPSHOT – continued

- staff should always explore the underlying reasons for aggression and look at what the child/ren are trying to communicate through aggressive behaviour and language;

- where necessary, a child should be removed from the other children and stay with a practitioner until ready to rejoin the group.

The setting manager explained the strategies to the parents and they arranged to meet again in a fortnight to review progress. During this follow-up meeting, the mothers reported that their children were now much happier and the setting manager described the improvements staff had noticed in the nature of garden play. Both parties agreed to remain vigilant about garden play and how it affected the children.

This snapshot shows the value of:

- *Listening to a complaint and making every effort to resolve it informally.*

- *Explaining to parents your reasons for a particular policy or procedure (in this case, the reasons for allowing lots of 'free play' in the garden).*

- *Giving credence to a parent's concerns and coming up with strategies to address those concerns.*

- *Being proactive in keeping parents informed.*

- *Getting feedback from parents as to whether or not the situation has been resolved to their satisfaction.*

TRY THIS

Treats and parties

Social events can be very useful in helping to form positive links with parents. The following occasions can all be used as an excuse for a party:

- religious festivals/celebrations
- performances/concerts
- summer picnics
- nature walks
- swimming trips
- a leaving party for children moving on to 'big school'
- outings to places of interest.

CURRICULUM GUIDANCE

Parent partnerships

The more information and support parents receive, the more confidence they will have when it comes to entrusting their child to your care. Successful partnerships between parents and setting help children towards the following PSED goals:

Separate from main carer with support (yellow ss);

Separate from main carer with confidence (blue ss);

Have a sense of self as a member of different communities (green ss);

Feel safe and secure and demonstrate a sense of trust (yellow ss);

Form good relationships with adults and peers (ELG).

Starting and ending a session

Saying goodbye to Mum or Dad, sorting out pegs, coats and lunchboxes, the excitement of waiting to be collected... Arriving at the setting and going home time need careful handling if they are not to turn into emotional flashpoints.

The chapter is divided into three sections:

- Starting the session
- Registration
- Ending the session.

Starting the session

Establishing routines, forward planning and preparation are the keys to a successful start.

Preparing yourself

Before you open the doors, double-check your appearance. If you feel happy with how you look, you will come across as much more confident and approachable. Even if you are not feeling your best, try to smile and present a warm, positive front. Never underestimate your role in setting the tone for the rest of the session, particularly if you are one of the staff members greeting the children and their parents.

As part of working on your own manner, watch out for the temptation to 'mirror' a child's mood when they first arrive. Mimicking tears or a cross face shows empathy, but it's not always the best way of lifting a child out of their mood. Try to keep your own facial reaction cheerful while you sort out whatever is upsetting the child.

Dropping-off time

For parents who don't come into the setting, dropping-off time may be their only chance to form impressions of you and your relationship with their child. It can be difficult for parents to accept that the grumpy or anxious three year old they brought to nursery went on to have a happy and productive morning, once they had settled. If you can provide a reassuring routine and create a welcoming atmosphere, parents will at least go away feeling that their child is in good hands.

Try to ensure that every child and their parent are greeted as they arrive. Dropping-off time is a useful opportunity to communicate with the parent and gather any information that they may be willing to pass on; for example, is the child excited about a special event happening later in the day? Has the child had a bad night or refused to eat breakfast? If you feel that all staff need to know about something the parents have passed on, make a note on the staff notice board (do, however, bear in mind that the notice board, while not intended for open access, is also not completely confidential). If you feel that a child is not well enough to cope with the session, or has an infectious illness such as conjunctivitis, you may have to ask the parent to take the child home. This can be difficult, particularly when parents are working. If parents challenge you, remind yourself (and, if necessary, the parent) that the needs of the child and the rest of the group are paramount. Be sympathetic and courteous, but stand firm.

SNAPSHOT – the mouse in the coat

As soon as Terri arrived in the setting, her key worker could tell that she was not her usual self.

> *'She's been fussing about her coat all the way here, and there's nothing wrong with it,'* said her father.
>
> *'I've got something in my coat and it's scratching me,'* responded Terri, tearfully.

The key worker made soothing noises to Terri and then turned away to deal with another child. Terri wriggled out of her coat by herself and her father hung it up. She was not very settled throughout the morning and when it was time to go outside, she did not want to put on her coat. Her key worker insisted on her wearing the coat as it was a cold day, and when Terri still refused to touch it, the key worker lifted it off her peg. To her horror, a small brown mouse scuttled out of the lining of the sleeve and shot off into the garden. Fortunately, Terri got over the shock quite quickly and when her father came to collect her, she took great delight in telling him all about the little brown mouse who lived in her coat. For Terri's key worker, the incident of 'the mouse in the coat' proved to be a learning experience. She admitted to herself that she should have listened more carefully to Terri and made a mental note to address this in the future.

This snapshot shows the value of:

- *Always taking a child's concerns seriously: had the practitioner given more attention to Terri, she might have discovered the mouse and saved the child an anxious morning.*

- *Constant self-assessment: Terri's key worker thought through the incident and looked at what she could learn to improve her practice.*

Cloakroom routines

How you organize your cloakroom routine will depend on the size and nature of your setting, the time of day your children arrive and whether you have a set arrival time or a staggered start. When planning your cloakroom routine, bear in mind the following:

- Encourage children to take off their coats and hang them up by themselves. This can be a useful moment to show parents just how much their children can manage by themselves.

- Greet each child and give them your undivided attention for a minute or two (see *TRY THIS – greetings role play*, page 51). If you have children whose home language is not English, ask the child and the parents to teach you how to greet them in their own language.

- Remind children where to put boots, lunchboxes, items from home and anything else they might have brought with them.

- If a child has had a long journey or has difficulties with the toilet, encourage them to go once they have taken off their coat.

- Some practitioners find it useful to have a point at which both they and the parent are clear that the setting has now taken over responsibility for the child. Encouraging the child to say a proper 'goodbye' to their parent makes a good marker. Asking parents to sign the Parents register (see page 56) also provides written documentation that the parent has delivered their child and the setting is now responsible for that child.

- Ensure that your cloakroom facilities are suitable for any child with disabilities. Check all entrances and exits and make sure that there is adequate access to the pegs, the boot rack and the toilets.

TRY THIS

Naming pegs

Although a colour or picture is useful for helping children to recognize their pegs, it is also a good idea to add name labels. The daily opportunity to see their name in writing will help children with name recognition.

TRY THIS

Greetings role play

Plan a set routine for greeting each child individually, for example:

- get down to the child's level
- encourage the child to look at you
- exchange greetings

    'Good morning, Jacob'

    'Good morning, Miss Hayley'

- have a quick chat about the child's journey/the weather/what they are wearing
- if you wish, shake hands while exchanging your greeting.

Practise the routine at other times of the day. Most children enjoy the challenge of acting out what they do when they arrive at the start of a session. Apart from providing an established routine for the child's arrival, the 'greetings' role play will help children to develop a valuable social skill.

TRY THIS

See-through bags

Clear plastic bags with handles make a useful means of storage for boots, spare clothes, suncream and sun hats. Stick a name label on each bag and hang it on the child's peg. You can then easily check whether or not the children have the things they need with them. As with any plastic bags, keep a close eye on safety.

CURRICULUM GUIDANCE

Dropping off/cloakroom routines

Carefully managing the child's arrival has an important role to play in the following PSED goals:

Separate from main carer with support/Feel safe and secure and demonstrate a sense of trust (yellow ss);

Separate from main carer with confidence (blue ss);

Have a sense of self as a member of different communities (green ss).

Demonstrate flexibility and adapt their behaviour to different events, social situations and changes in routine (blue ss);

Starting off

The children have arrived, their belongings have been put away and they are starting to settle in. There are various possible ways to organize the start of a session:

- **The small group start**: small, adult-initiated group activities can be a useful way to start the day, particularly during the first few weeks of a new year. If the group is generally unsettled, the small group format can also be used for calming the children, making them feel more secure and giving them some direction.

- **The large group start**: a large group can be difficult to organize if your children arrive at different times. It is also harder to handle younger children and unsettled children in a large group. The large group can, however, be useful when you need to give a message to all the children, for example, talking to them about a visit from the photographer.

- **The 'free choice' start**: once children are familiar with the setting, a free choice activity period enables them to take stock and settle down in their own time. The free choice period can also be a useful way to start the session if you have a staggered arrival time, or need to accommodate parents who find it difficult to deliver their children at a set time.

The following routine is just one possible way of easing the children into a free choice period at the start of a session:

- The staff member on duty in the cloakroom directs the child to their key worker or a second staff member waiting to receive the children in the setting.

- The key worker greets the child.

- The key worker helps the child to register (see *Self registration*, page 58) and, if necessary, reminds them to put away any belongings.

- The key worker helps the child decide what they would like to do.

It is essential that all staff observe the group closely as some children may need a little reminder of how to conduct themselves in the setting. If a child does appear to need direction, step in and give some support. It is, however, important to avoid pushing the child to 'do' something. Always remember that chatting with other children or staff, observing what is happening and generally orientating themselves are all valid and valuable activities.

INFORMATION LINKS

For information on:

■ settling new children at the start of the session see pages 13–24.

■ observing children at the start of the session see page 24.

CURRICULUM GUIDANCE

Starting the session

Planning a free choice activity period and encouraging social interaction at the start of the session helps towards a number of goals, including:

Initiate interactions with other people (PSED/green ss);

Show increasing independence in selecting and carrying out activities (PSED/blue ss);

Display high levels of involvement in activities/Persist for extended periods of time at an activity of their choosing (PSED/green ss);

Maintain attention, concentrate and sit quietly when appropriate (PSED/ELG);

Relate and make attachments to members of their groups (PSED/yellow ss);

Form good relationships with adults and peers (PSED/ELG);

Use words and/or gestures, including body language such as eye contact and facial expression, to communicate (CLL/yellow ss);

Have emerging self-confidence to speak to others about wants and interests/Initiate conversation, attend to and take account of what others say ... (CLL/green ss);

Interact with others, negotiating plans and activities and taking turns in conversation (CLL/ELG)

Safety at the start of the session

It is vital that all adults in the setting are aware of safety at the start of the day. With so many comings and goings, trips and accidents can easily happen. There is also the risk of a child wandering off if neither parent nor staff are clear about who is supervising. Be vigilant, develop eyes in the back of your head and never forget the importance of close supervision at all times.

If possible, have a set period when your door is open to receive children. During that time, a staff member should always be on duty and keeping a close eye on the door. All staff should be informed when the door is opened, and when it has been closed and secured. From that point onwards, people should only be able to gain access to the setting by ringing on a doorbell. The aim of securing the door is to prevent children from getting out and unwanted visitors from getting in. However, adults must be able to evacuate children quickly in the event of an emergency. If you are in any doubt about balancing security and accessibility, seek expert advice.

If you want to provide free garden access at all times (see pages 105–6), apply the above procedures to securing any entrances and exits to your garden.

INFORMATION LINKS

For more on:

■ safety issues in your Policy and Procedures document see pages 30 and 32.

Punctuality

Be as flexible as possible about punctuality and plan a start to the day that accommodates children arriving at different times (see *Starting off/The 'free choice' start*, page 52). If you start the session at a set time, a sympathetic response to occasional lateness or lateness with good reason will be much appreciated by the parent. Working parents and parents who care for relatives and/or younger siblings can find it difficult to be punctual all the time – and none of us has control over the traffic!

If persistent lateness becomes disruptive for the child, you may decide to raise the issue with the parents. Do so in a light-hearted manner – if possible, slip it into the conversation and be ready to be sympathetic and flexible if the parent chooses to give you reasons for their lack of punctuality. If necessary, explain that many older children hate being late (something that their parents may not realize) and that it can be much more difficult for a child to settle if they miss out on the first part of the session.

TRY THIS

A 'Punctuality Poster'

If you don't want to confront individuals over punctuality, try putting up a light-hearted poster with bright, positive motifs such as smiley faces. Go for a plea rather than a stern approach:

We love to see your children
They brighten up our day
And if you bring them here on time
The sooner we can play.

Observation notes

Observation during the start of a session gives you an initial opportunity to assess each child's mood and level of well being, how easily they separate from their parents and how quickly they adjust to the atmosphere and routines of the setting.

- When parents drop off their children, take a good look at each child and make a mental note of how they come across. Are they unusually pale, tired, quiet or unsettled? If a child does not seem to be him or herself, tactfully ask the parents if there is any factor that might have affected their child, such as a disturbed night. You may also be able to pick up on a child's mood and the behavioural challenges that might lie ahead.

- Observe how the children manage cloakroom routines. Can they find their pegs, take off their coats and put away their belongings? Are they able to do all these things independently or do they still need physical help and/or reminders? Assess your observations and give certain children more practice with cloakroom routines if necessary.

- Once children are in the setting and the session has begun, observe as much as possible during the first 30 minutes or so. The start of the session is an important time for assessing which children might need careful handling and support. Observe how quickly the children remember the routines of the setting and choose something to do, or settle into a planned group activity. Look out in particular for the child who is unusually forgetful about routines such as putting an activity back – this can be a sign that the child is unsettled and may need extra attention.

- If you start with a free choice activity period, observe the particular activities a child chooses. Children will often go for their favourite activity first thing and you can learn a lot about a child's interests, talents, likes and dislikes and what are the most and least popular activities in the setting.

- During a free choice activity period, keep an eye out for the child who starts every session with the same self-chosen routine of activities. While this is not a problem in itself, if you feel that they are using their routine as a 'security blanket', it may be a good idea to step in and gently introduce some new experiences.

- Observing children at the start of the session may contribute to the following points in the **Foundation Profile** assessment scales:
  - how children separate from their parent

    Emotional development 1 and 2
  - how children participate in groups and individual activities

    Disposition and attitudes 1, 3, 5, 6, 7, 8, 9

    Social development 1, 2, 3, 4, 5

    Language for communication and thinking 1, 2, 3, 5, 6, 7, 8, 9
  - how children manage cloakroom routines

    Dispositions and attitudes 2

For a summary of different observational approaches, see page 4.

Registration

All early years settings are required to register the arrival and departure times for both children and staff, plus any students or adult helpers. All staff need to know how many adults and children are in the setting, who is absent, and be able to access that information quickly in the event of an emergency. You also need to keep ongoing records of attendance throughout a child's time in the setting.

It is a good idea to have parents or carers sign and register the time that they have delivered their child to the setting. Place a Parents register by the entrance to the setting. The staff on duty in the cloakroom can remind parents to sign if necessary, and the Parents register can then be checked against the main register.

To ensure that the register is filled in accurately, two staff members should take responsibility for registration. One adult fills in the register, the other double-checks that it is accurate. If you use this system, it is preferable for the roles of 'register-taker' and 'checker' to be permanent. The more established the routine, the less likely it is for someone to forget or make an error. It is also important to keep the register in a designated and accessible place so that it is easily available if you have to exit the building in an emergency. If you have different groups of children on different days, always remember to check that you are filling in the correct register for the session.

Although double-checking should be incorporated into any registration technique, the routine you use will depend on whether you start your day with a free choice activity period, a large group activity or a series of small group activities.

Registering during free choice time

Registering children during a free choice activity period takes vigilance! The role of the checker is particularly important in making sure that no child has been missed. The following sample routine is based on a setting where all the children arrive at approximately the same time. It illustrates the 'register-taker/checker' approach in operation and can be adopted as it stands or adjusted to suit the particular structure of your setting.

- The register-taker stands near the entrance with the register and marks each child present as they come into the setting. This staff member focuses solely on the register, with other staff taking responsibility for settling the children. All staff make sure that the register-taker is not distracted and the children understand that he or she should not be disturbed until registration has finished.

- Once the register has been filled in, a second staff member double-checks that it has been completed accurately, and checks the numbers against the Parents register. Ideally, the setting manager should be the 'checker' as they have overall responsibility for the children's welfare.

- The checker writes the number of children present in large numbers on a white board. The white board is displayed so that it can clearly be seen by all adults, but is out of reach of the children. The names of absent children are also written alongside the number.

■ The checker double-checks that the numbers on the white board are accurate by adding the total number of children marked present in the register to the number of absent children, and matching the total against the overall size of the group.

■ When a child leaves early or arrives late, the checker ensures that the child's key worker has adjusted both the register and the white board.

TRY THIS

Important contacts

The front of your register is a good place to keep important contact details, for example, the local police, hospital A&E department, NHS Direct, local health visitor, local Pre-school Learning Alliance office and Social Services family team for your area.

Registering in groups

It can be easier to take the register when you start the day with group activities as all the children will be 'in one place'. In a large group, the register-taker can simply stand by the group and complete the register. Alternatively, the practitioner leading the group activity can take the register by asking each child to answer when their name is called. Once the register has been taken, it should be double-checked by a designated checker (see above).

If you start the session with the children participating in lots of separate, adult-led small group activities, the register-taker can wander around the groups, filling in the register. Alternatively, if the children start every session in the same little group with their key worker, each key worker can take responsibility for registering their own group. In this instance, the role of the checker is doubly important in checking that everyone has registered their children correctly and transferring the names to the main register.

TRY THIS

Register codes

Register codes can be very useful for alerting staff to patterns of absence. Try the following:

S = sick

U = unexplained absence

H = child away on holiday

X = days/sessions when child not attending

PH = public holiday/setting holiday.

TRY THIS

Helping with the register

If you take the register in a group, ask the children to help you. This means that they do not have to wait with nothing to do while you work your way through all the names. Try the following ideas:

■ Get all the children to join in with singing the register: 'Gemma, Gemma, Gemma are you here today?'

■ Hold up name cards or photos, one at a time. Ask the children to stand up when they recognize their name/photo so you can mark them in the register (get a supporting practitioner to help children who need support).

■ If your group is not too big, distribute name cards amongst the children and ask them to read out the names, one at a time. Tell the children to listen carefully and jump up when they hear their name so that you can mark them in the register.

Self registration

Although the adults in the setting should take responsibility for registration, the children can also register themselves. Apart from giving the children the opportunity to recognize their names and participate in a daily routine, self registration gives you yet another means of checking who is present. Try the following technique:

■ Make laminated name cards for each child and stick a magnetic strip on the back.

■ Attach the names to a magnetic board.

■ Attach laminated passport photos of each child to a second magnetic board.

■ As each child enters the setting, a practitioner sitting beside the board helps them to find their name, remove it and place it under their photo.

■ Watch out for children putting their names upside down.

■ Encourage children to remember to add or remove their names if they arrive late or leave early.

CURRICULUM GUIDANCE

Self registration

Implementing a self-registration system and involving children with the register can help towards the following PSED goals:

Have a sense of belonging (blue ss);

Have a sense of self as a member of different communities (green ss).

Ending the session

A carefully planned 'going home' routine is very settling for the child. At this young age, children have little real sense of the passage of time and they need a sequential routine in order to orientate themselves. If they know that snack time is followed by outdoor play, outdoor play is followed by free activity time and free activities are followed by a going home group, it will give them the security of knowing when they will be collected.

How you organize the end of the session will depend on the nature of your setting. With a staggered collection time, a free choice activity period works well. If you have a set collection time, group activities can be the easiest way to manage your end of session routines. If you have some children leaving at the end of the morning and others staying on for the afternoon, you may choose to split into a 'lunchtime' group and a 'going home' group.

Free choice activity time

Free choice activities at the end of a session need careful supervision. Some children do not find it easy to settle to an activity when they are anticipating their parents' arrival. Be ready to play a short game with a small group of children. Choose simple activities that can be cleared away quickly and don't have to be finished off. For example:

- drawing with a single pencil rather than using a full set of crayon
- doing a small tray puzzle rather than a large floor puzzle
- playing a quick, simple card game such as Snap, rather than a complex game such as Lotto
- completing a lacing card rather than playing with the Duplo
- sharing a book of short nursery rhymes with children, rather than embarking on a full length story.

Maintain your 'tidying-up' routine and help the child to clear away their activity once their parent arrives. If necessary, explain to parents why you are asking them to wait for a moment while their child tidies up after themselves. If a child is in the middle of an activity such as lacing, show them how to put it on a shelf with their name card so that they can finish it tomorrow.

If your cloakroom is separate from the main part of the setting, it can be less unsettling for the children if the parents stay in the cloakroom. The staff member on duty can then call the child to the cloakroom when their parent has arrived. If you have parents collecting their children directly from the activity area, watch out for the child who is unsettled by the arrival of their parent and disrupts the rest of the group. Try to arrange an earlier collection time or ask the parent to wait outside the main part of the setting while you bring the child to them. Watch out also for the child who becomes upset watching other children enthusiastically greeting their mums/dads/childminders while they remain uncollected. Give the child lots of special attention, and consider whether it would work for your setting to ask all parents to stay in the cloakroom area.

'Going home' groups

If your children are generally settled during group activities, a well-managed group activity enables staff to 'keep tabs' on all the children, prior to collection time. With a large group, have a supporting practitioner on hand to keep the children settled and help them gather their belongings after they leave the group. As with free choice activities, it can be easier to keep the group calm if parents stay in the cloakroom while a staff member calls children from the group. This also enables you to stagger the flow of children coming into the cloakroom. Aim to start the group about ten minutes before collection time. This gives the children a chance to settle before they are collected. Choose light-hearted activities and plan a long list of short activities rather than just two or three longer ones. For example:

- reading a short story
- songs/rhymes
- singing games such as 'five currant buns'
- looking at an item/picture.

Time the group carefully to make sure that activities, such as reading a story, are finished before the parents start arriving. You can then keep the rest of the group occupied with rhymes, songs and finger plays as the children are collected.

End of session routines

Carefully thought-out routines are the foundation for a calm and happy end to the session. When planning your end of session routines, bear in mind the following:

- **Taking home 'work'**: paintings, drawings and craft can be set out on a table or placed in named trays, ready for the children to collect. If you end the session with the children participating in a large group activity, another option is for a staff member to place the work under each child's chair, ready for them to pick up when they are collected. If the group is small and settled, hand each child their work for them to put under their chair themselves.

■ **Toys from home**: if you encourage children to bring in toys from home, it is useful to keep them in a special toy box. Children can then be reminded to collect their toy at the end of the session. Being firm about putting toys in the toy box when not in use will lessen the likelihood of things getting lost. Special items brought in for a project should be kept out of the children's reach and preferably returned directly to the parent.

■ **Putting on coats**: encourage children to put on their coats independently. If your cloakroom area is small, it can be easier to organize the children putting on their coats before the parents arrive.

TRY THIS

Putting on coats

Introduce a technique for putting on coats and practise it with the children:

■ Lay the coat on the floor with the lining facing upwards. Ask the children to stand with toes touching the collar, put their arms deep inside the armholes and lift the coat up and over their heads.

■ Put the coat over the back of a chair. Ask a child to sit on the chair and slip their arms through the armholes before standing up.

■ **Saying goodbye**: saying goodbye to the staff member supervising the cloakroom marks the end of the session, and the point at which the parent takes over responsibility for the child, as well as helping the child to develop a useful social skill. Practise a 'goodbye' routine similar to your 'greeting' routine (see page 51).

■ **Remembering everything**: an established routine will help children to remember everything – and help you to check that nothing has been forgotten. For example, when a child is called to go the cloakroom, they:

- put away their sitting mat/chair

- collect drawings from their tray/the 'work' table

- fetch their toy from the toy box

- put on their coat

- pick up their lunchbox

- say goodbye to their key worker/staff on duty in the cloakroom

- leave with their parent.

Some children can end up with a lot to remember and may need support. Nevertheless, a routine along these lines will help to create a calm end to the session, as well as ensuring that lunchboxes, toys and other precious items end up where they should be.

CURRICULUM GUIDANCE

Ending the session

Helping children adjust to the setting, establishing routines for ending the session and reminding children of appropriate behaviour can help towards the following PSED goals:

> *Demonstrate flexibility and adapt their behaviour to different events, social situations and changes in routine* (blue ss);

> *Have an awareness of the boundaries set and behavioural expectations within the setting* (green ss).

Showing children techniques for putting on coats helps towards the following PSED goal:

> *Dress and undress independently ...* (ELG).

Punctuality and the non-collection of children

Parents who are late collecting their children can cause the child quite a lot of distress. If you feel you need to raise the issue with parents who are persistently late, adopt a similar approach to that suggested for late arrivals (see page 54) – with the addition of emphasizing how upset children can become when their parents do not arrive to collect them. If relevant, charging for the time overrun can help bring home to parents the importance of punctuality. Do, however, make sure you always have the children ready to go at collection time. You will not be in a good position to address punctuality if you are often late yourself, and parents are more likely to arrive on time if they know that their children will be ready and waiting.

Very occasionally, a child remains uncollected. In this instance, it is useful to have a written policy to follow. When compiling your Collection policy, aim to cover the following points:

- Parents must provide contact details, the name and contact details of any other adults authorized to collect the child and details of an emergency contact.

- The setting should be informed of any court orders preventing a particular adult from having contact with a child.

- Parents must inform the setting if anyone other than the usual person is collecting the child, and fill in/sign the Collection book.

- If parents cannot be contacted by the usual means on a particular day, they should record how they can be contacted in the Collection book.

■ A child will not be allowed to leave with anyone other than the adult/s who usually collect the child, unless parents have informed the setting in writing/filled in the Collection book.

■ Describe procedures for the non-collection of children. For example:

– Every effort will be made to contact the child's parents

– Failing that, the emergency contact/other authorized adults will be contacted

– When staff are no longer able to care for the child in the setting, the local Pre-school Learning Alliance office will be contacted to advise staff (give contact details). The local authority Social Services department will also be contacted (give contact details)

– Throughout the procedure, staff will make continuous efforts to contact parents/other authorized adults. The child will, at all times, be in the care of at least two staff members

– A written report will be made of the incident

– The setting reserves the right to charge parents for the cost of care (if relevant).

Very occasionally, you may have to deal with an unauthorized adult turning up to collect a child. Try to contact the parents or carers to inform them of the situation and on no account let the child leave with the adult. If the worst happens and things become unpleasant, don't be afraid to lock the doors and call the police. These situations are always upsetting to deal with, but do your best to put on a calm front and reassure the child that you are in charge of things.

SNAPSHOT – calling the right child

Nathan was normally collected by his dad, but today Grandma was taking him shopping and he was excitedly waiting for her to arrive. When the staff member on cloakroom duty called Nathan to collect his belongings, he hurried to the cloakroom, almost forgetting to pick up his snack box. A few minutes later, another staff member spotted Nathan crying by himself in a corner of the cloakroom. Fortunately, his grandma arrived at that very moment. The staff explained their error and Nathan soon forgot his tears. As a result of the incident, the staff reviewed their collection procedures and agreed on the following:

■ The staff member on duty should check the Collection book as a matter of course, and make a written note of any children who are being collected by a different person.

■ If the adult is unknown to the setting, the staff member should introduce him or herself, ask for the person's identity and check which child they are collecting.

■ The staff member should check that every adult and child have seen each other.

SNAPSHOT – continued

- Staff should keep a constant check on the Parents register to ensure that parents sign as they collect their child.
- Staff must be vigilant and aware of all children at all times.

This snapshot shows the value of:

- Assessing an unfortunate incident as a team and reviewing procedures to prevent such an incident from occurring again.

Safety at the end of the session

As with arrival time, going home is an exciting event and close supervision is important. Try to make sure that every child is 'handed' to the parent and check that the child and the parent have actually seen each other. Remember also that you need to record the times at which children, staff, students and adult helpers leave the setting.

If your setting is on a busy road, keep on emphasizing the importance of road safety with:

- safety posters
- information in your 'Policy and Procedures' document
- reminders at parents meetings.

Communications with parents

Try to give each parent a moment or two as they collect their child. Most will want to know how their child has got on and sharing a positive little anecdote can really brighten up their day. There may also be information that you need to pass on to parents, quite

TRY THIS

Space for parents

Collection time is a social event for many parents. Forming friendships with other adults is important, particularly for home-based parents and carers. It is also very helpful to the children's own friendships if families organize social events with one another. If at all possible, create a space where parents can chat to one another and make parents feel that they are welcome to linger. (Although be vigilant about safety – it can be easy for a parent to lose track of a child when they are busy chatting!)

Observation notes

Supervision and safety should be your first priority at the end of the session; for example, making sure the children collect all their belongings, cope with the cloakroom and end up safely reunited with whoever is collecting them. Targeted observation at the end of the session should be carried out by a practitioner who is not involved in supervising or supporting the children.

- Observe whether or not the children remember their belongings and follow routines such as putting away their chairs, finding their pegs and putting on their coats. Are they able to do these things independently or do they need support?

- Assess your end of session routines – for example, are the children managing to find their pictures/toys/lunchboxes to take home? Could the routines be made more straightforward for the children to remember and follow?

- Observe any children with special needs. How do they cope with the end of session routines? Are there any changes or adjustments that could be made to better meet their particular needs?

- Observe how the children react when they are picked up. Be ready to give extra support if certain children get very excited or even start to behave negatively when their parents arrive. Discreetly observe how parents respond to and link with their child. The end of the session is a good moment to pick up some clues as to a child/parent relationship and how it might impact on the child's behaviour in the setting. Do, however, bear in mind that such observations will only give you a quick snapshot – try to keep any snippets of information in perspective. It is also essential that parents are not made to feel watched in any way.

- Observing children as they put on their coats at the end of the session may contribute to the following point in the **Foundation Profile** assessment scales:

  – *Disposition and attitudes 2.*

For a summary of different observational approaches, see page 4.

apart from discussing any concerns or reassuring parents if their child seems unusually tired or overwrought. Ensure that nothing is forgotten by hanging a notice board near the entrance to the cloakroom and making a note of anything you need to discuss with individual parents. This might include signing the Accident book or mentioning that a child seems unsettled. Although parents and visitors shouldn't have access to the board, bear in mind that it will not be confidential. Make sure you only write up reminders, rather than personal details.

Working with groups of children

Six small children sitting in a circle, engaged in a carefully planned activity and waiting patiently for their turn ... a flurry of tissue paper, gluey fingers and happy excited artists ... a cosy huddle of children, gathered at their teacher's knee and listening to a story... Every group activity in the early years setting is different, depending on the nature of the activity, how you choose to manage it and the personality of the children. With so many possibilities, it is important to meet the challenges of the group activity with as much planning, preparation and enthusiasm as you can muster!

The chapter is divided into three sections:

- Planning and preparation

- Implementing planned group activities

- Child participation.

Planning and preparation

Preparation is key to the success of a group activity. This section looks at some of the areas you need to cover as you plan your activities.

Group size

The number of children in your group will depend on the purpose of the activity and the age and personality of the children. In the early years setting, any more than ten children is challenging to manage effectively, particularly at the beginning of the year when new children are still settling. It can be tempting to make a group as large as possible – group activities keep children 'usefully' occupied and a large group enables you to introduce an activity to lots of children at once. However, children will usually gain much more from being in a small group. If you can keep numbers down to three or four, you can give far greater individual attention to each child. It is also easier to monitor the children's responses and assess their learning in a small group.

Activities for large groups/circle time

The overall aim of a large group activity or circle time will usually differ from the small group. The large group is more likely to contain a range of ages, particularly in the pre-school setting. This in itself will affect the activities you choose to undertake. The following activities work well with a large group and they are also easy to adapt for a range of ages:

- reading/telling stories

- songs, nursery and action rhymes

- clapping activities/percussion groups

- talking about feelings linked to an event or story

- reinforcement of routines such as putting books back in the book corner

- giving news

- short discussion about a story, event, visit, activity

- introducing new resources

- large group role play.

INFORMATION LINKS

For more on:

- circle time see Further Reading.

Activities for small groups

With the small group, you can choose children of a similar ability level. This makes it a better environment for introducing activities with specific learning objectives. The following work well in small groups:

- exploring a theme/topic
- art/craft

- turn-taking activities/games/physical development activities
- role play
- exploring sounds/letters/early reading activities
- writing activities
- exploring mathematical concepts.

Group arrangement: large groups/circle time

The smooth running of a large group is partly dependent on its physical format, particularly if you have a number of unsettled children. Choose a formal arrangement such as a semi-circle or a wide U with space on either side of the group leader. Both the semi-circle and the U shape enable all the children to see the adult. They also incorporate space on either side of the group leader, allowing her to move a child next to her without having to disturb other children.

It is also well worth providing each child with their own clearly defined space in the form of a chair or a sitting mat. If you have children who tend to distract one another, sitting on chairs is the best choice. Crowding in a huddle on the carpet is cosy, but hard to manage with more than six or so children.

Group arrangement: small groups

Small groups are usually easier to manage than large groups. For this reason, you can be more flexible, choosing different formats to suit different activities.

- **Chairs and table**: a table is essential if you are using resources, or if you want the children to work on paper. Ask the children to keep their hands off the table while you show the activity. This ensures that everyone can see and discourages children from playing with the resources while you are still introducing them.

- **The floor**: some activities work better on the floor, for example, a large game. Use a floor mat to define the working area. Use small sitting mats to show children where to sit and give them their own space.

- **The book corner**: squashing cosily into the book corner can work well for small story or rhyme groups. As long as children are not disturbing one another, let them sit however they wish.

- **Other areas of the setting**: choose different areas of the setting to reflect the nature of the activity, for example, an appropriate play setting such as the home corner for role play. Find a part of the setting where the acoustics are best for singing, or the lighting is particularly good for drawing, and try singing and drawing outside.

■ **Avoiding distractions**: a number of children will probably be busy elsewhere in the setting while you conduct your small group. If you are introducing something that involves listening closely, find a quiet space. Position your table and chairs so that the children are facing you, with their backs to the main body of the room. As well as shielding the children from possible distractions, this arrangement enables you to keep an eye on the rest of the room (although the group activity is your priority, all staff should constantly be aware of all other children).

■ **Special needs**: always consider children with special needs and disabilities when planning where to hold your group. For example, playing a game on the floor would not be appropriate for a wheelchair user.

Planning group activities

As with any aspect of the early years setting, planning and preparation for your group activity is essential. The following checklist covers the areas you need to consider:

■ **Timetabling and timings**: decide when to hold your group activity and approximately how long you expect it to last. This will depend on the purpose of the activity and the attention span of the children. If you want to introduce a new skill or concept, choose a time when your children are settled. Use a large group to signal the start of the morning or afternoon and bring everyone together at the end of the session. Although it is important to be flexible over timings, remember that many children struggle to concentrate for longer than 15 minutes, particularly in a large group.

■ **Aims**: have a clear idea of your aims. Apart from specific learning objectives, group activities can have a number of purposes, for example:

– giving direction to unsettled children;

– reinforcing a routine;

– starting/ending a session;

– developing the ability to co-operate within a group (listening, contributing to discussion, turn-taking).

■ **Who to include**: some small group activities are part of an ongoing process. For example, if you want to introduce reading simple words to certain children, there is a number of skills they will need to have covered. Check records to ensure that every child in the group is ready for the new activity – if something is too difficult for them, you will lose their attention. Creative activities such as craft or role play work particularly well with a mix of ages and/or abilities. When choosing children for such activities, consider what combination of personalities is likely to bring out the best in each child. If you have a spread of ages, try to include children who know what they are doing – the younger and/or less experienced child can learn a huge amount from observing others.

■ **Content**: make a list of the activities you plan to do within the group session. The following format works well for a large group/circle time:

- familiar rhyme/song

- story or book, connected to a topic or to reflect a particular personal, social or emotional issue

- discussion about the story

- sharing news

- familiar rhyme/song.

If you have a range of ages in your group, lean towards content that is appropriate for younger children. Older ones can always join in activities for younger ones, whereas you will lose the attention of the little ones very quickly if the content is too far above them. Redress the balance with lots of age-specific small group activities for older ones.

■ **Resources**: prepare a list of the resources you will need for your group activity and make sure you have everything to hand. If you are planning to read a story towards the end of the group session, don't forget to put it out before you begin. The unplanned delay while you make a quick dash to the book corner can be all it takes to unsettle the children.

■ **Practising**: careful preparation will make you feel more confident – a confidence that will communicate itself to the children. Practise reading a story and try out special voices (although bear in mind that some children can be unnerved when a safe, familiar adult suddenly changes character). If you are introducing a new rhyme or song, make sure you are word perfect. Having the content of the activity at your fingertips will free you up to focus on the children and their reactions.

■ **Flexibility**: although a carefully structured plan is important, you do need to be flexible. If children are not taking off on a particular activity, draw it to a close and move on. If the children are inspired, give them a free rein. If one particular activity in your plan takes up more time than you expected, don't be afraid to cancel the other items on the agenda – you can always save them for another day.

SNAPSHOT – preparing for a group

A student practitioner had planned a sticking activity with Sanjeet, Hannah and Nathan. In readiness for the activity, she had put out a pot of glue, some saucers and three glue spatulas. The student explained the activity to the children and then started to pour glue into the saucers. Before she could finish, Sanjeet asked for help with choosing shapes to stick onto his background. Left without her own glue, Hannah leant across to borrow Nathan's and managed to drip glue across his picture. Nathan and Hannah started to argue and the student had to stop and help them clear up. Later that day, the student discussed the activity with her mentor. The mentor pointed out that the incident presented a good opportunity for the children to share equipment and resources, and that the student could help them to do this if a similar opportunity arose.

This snapshot shows the value of:

■ *Preparing resources in advance to enable activities to run smoothly.*

■ *Making the most of any opportunity to encourage children to negotiate, problem solve and co-operate with one another.*

CURRICULUM GUIDANCE

Planning and preparation

A well-planned and managed group activity helps the children develop positive attitudes to learning. This contributes to many PSED goals, including:

> *Show curiosity/Have a positive approach to new experiences* (yellow ss);

> *Continue to be interested, excited and motivated to learn* (ELG).

Implementing planned group activities

Once you have completed your planning and preparation, the next step to consider is how you implement the activity.

Starting off

The large group activity

The golden rule for starting any activity is to offer something enticing from the beginning. Children like routine and knowing what to expect can help them settle in a large group activity. A familiar rhyme or song makes a quick, simple and appealing start. Accommodate older children who get bored with the same old rhymes by asking them to choose the next rhyme.

As much as possible, avoid gaps where nothing happens and never expect children to just sit and wait for others to join the activity. One way to avoid this is to have a 'staggered start'. Gather a few settled children who won't be thrown by constant interruptions and sing an action rhyme while staff help the rest of the children to join the group, one-by-one. As each child arrives, give them a welcoming smile and encourage them to join in with the rhyme. Choose rhymes with a series of short, separate actions. This enables you to pick up the thread if the rhyme is interrupted and keep going for as long as necessary. Another important element is the copycat action as this encourages the children to focus on you as the group leader. For example:

Everybody do this, do this, do this
Everybody do this, just like me

(with an accompanying action such as stamping, nodding, jumping).

Clap your hands, clap, clap clap
Clap your hands, oh clap, clap, clap

(continue with other actions such as *tap your toes* or *wiggle your fingers*)
Once all the children are seated, you can then move on to the main part of the activity.

The small group activity

Starting off a small group activity is a little different from starting off a large group activity. Whereas it is not realistic to expect large numbers of children to be completely still before you start, in a small group you can challenge them to be as quiet as mice and put their hands in their laps. Once the group is settled, attract their attention and entice them to look at you with an inviting statement: '*We are going to do a very special shape activity in our group today*'. Use your eyes and voice to add emphasis to your words. When you have gained the children's attention, you can then proceed with the activity. It is, however, important to make sure that the activity lives up to your introduction. If you suggest that you are going to do something interesting and then fail to deliver, the children will stop believing you!

TRY THIS

A quiet start

If you find that simply asking a large group to be quiet is not working, try ringing a bell, clapping your hands, singing '*quiet please*' or playing a few special chords on the piano. Talk to the children about the importance of being quiet at the start of a group and discuss which method they prefer you to use, and why.

TRY THIS

Something in a box

Spark interest in an activity by hiding the resources in a box. Start off the activity with a statement such as: '*I have something very interesting in my box today*'. This is guaranteed to grab the children's attention.

SNAPSHOT – pre-empting disruptions

Lots of children in the setting had colds and the demand for tissues was disrupting group activities. (When one child wanted a tissue, every child wanted a tissue!) A staff member decided to respond by having a nose-blowing session at the start of his small group activity. He invited each child to take a tissue from the box, blow their nose and put their tissue in the bin. He then placed the tissue box within easy reach of his chair. As the activity proceeded, it became obvious that Sasha needed another tissue. When the practitioner passed her the box, Anna also asked for a tissue. The practitioner reminded Anna that she had used a tissue at the start of the group. He also pointed out that she did not have a cold like Sasha and that she could have a tissue at the end of the activity if she still wanted one. He then proceeded quickly with the activity to distract Anna's attention away from the tissue box.

This snapshot shows the value of:

- *Working with the children's needs and interests – by incorporating nose blowing into the activity, the practitioner enabled the children to explore their interest in the tissue box.*

- *Watching out for repetitive behaviour patterns and planning ways to deal with them, in order to pre-empt disruptions.*

- *Organizing resources so they are near at hand (the practitioner placed the tissue box within easy reach of his chair in case it was needed again).*

Conducting the group activity

Managing large and small group activities draws on different skills. The presence of a supporting practitioner is also important, particularly with a large group.

Your role as a performer

While you don't have to be an Oscar-winning actor, you do need to produce a bit of a performance, particularly when managing large groups of children. Use voice, facial expression and body language to communicate that what you are saying is worth listening to. Work on your timing – when to pause for effect, when to change the tempo by moving on quickly to a new topic or question. Another useful trick is to 'sweep' the entire circle with your eyes. This helps you to keep tabs on the group as a whole, instead of just focusing on the few children in front of you.

Your role in the small group

With fewer children to deal with, conducting a small group activity is less about your skills as a performer and more about involving each child as an individual. The following pointers are of key importance when it comes to helping children engage with the activity or resources:

- Double-check that each child in the group is ready for the activity.

- Wherever possible, include children who work together in your group.

- Choose an area of the setting and seating plan to match the activity (see *Group arrangements*, pages 68–9).

- Plan the activity carefully and practise your delivery.

- Prepare thoroughly, making sure you have all props and resources within easy reach.

Asking questions

Asking questions can be quite a complex procedure. Bear in mind the following:

- Avoid throwing out a question to the whole group, unless you want to be bombarded with a chorus of answers. Focus instead on asking a specific child to answer a question. From about four onwards, you can introduce putting up hands.

- Avoid 'open-ended' questions such as: '*Can you tell the group about your holidays?*' For many children, the scope of this question is too wide for them to know where to begin, while the talkative child will not know where to end.

- Avoid 'closed' questions that do not encourage more than a yes/no answer, for example: '*Did you go to the beach on your holiday?*'

- Aim for questions that offer scope to expand, but within the limits of a specified topic, for example: '*Joseph, what did you do when you went to the beach?*'

- If you are inexperienced at asking questions in a group, try out the question on yourself before presenting it to the children. If the question leaves you wondering what element to focus on, it is probably too open-ended. If the only immediate answer is 'yes' or 'no', it is probably too closed.

Practitioner support

Always ask a supporting practitioner to join a large group, to help the children remain settled. If practitioners sit behind the children rather than within the circle, they will be able to see the children more clearly. It is also much easier for them to move to different parts of the circle without disrupting the group.

If you are the one taking the supporting role in a large group, be aware of the following:

- Your role is to be proactive in supporting the group leader; however interesting the activity, keep your attention on the children.

- Watch out for signals from the group leader that support is needed.

- Be ready to move round the circle to sit with children who are unsettled.

- Always operate quietly and discreetly, with minimum disruption to the group as a whole.

- Be ready to intercept a child who leaves the group (see *Wandering off*, pages 79–80).

Small groups can be conducted by a single person, although it is useful to be able to call upon a nearby practitioner if necessary. If you have support workers for children with special needs in your setting, they will also join the group along with the child they are supporting.

TRY THIS

Speaking quietly

Encourage children to listen more closely by using a quiet voice. The children will also start to imitate you and the group as a whole should become calmer.

CURRICULUM GUIDANCE

Asking questions

Questions are a useful tool for encouraging children to consider moral issues, helping towards the following PSED goal:

> *Understand what is right, what is wrong, and why (ELG).*

Asking questions provides children with a model for the questioning process, helping toward the following CLL goals:

> *Question why things happen, and give explanations* (blue ss);

> *Ask simple questions, often in the form of 'where' or 'what'* (green ss);

> *Sustain attentive listening, responding to what they have heard by relevant comments, questions or actions* (ELG).

Finishing the group activity/circle time

Once a group activity has finished, some children may need help in moving on to the next activity. Following a large group activity or circle time, it can be useful to avoid simply releasing the children *en masse* into the setting. If the group activity takes place prior to an organized event such as washing hands before lunch, check that there are practitioners ready to receive the children. Choose children who find it hard to sit in a group first, and send them off with clear instructions about where to go: *'James and Joshua, will you go to Miss Hayley in the cloakroom'*. Keep the rest of the children occupied with action rhymes until it is their turn to leave the group.

If the children are moving on to a free choice period, they may need some support in making a seamless transition from the adult-controlled environment of the group activity to the relative freedom of choosing time. The age and previous experience of each child in the group will have a bearing on how much support you offer. Children who are new to the setting or generally unsettled may not be able to cope with too much choice. Suggest one or two activities to each child and direct them towards something familiar: *'Can you find the crayons and paper in the writing corner?'* If you feel they need more support, direct them towards a practitioner: *'Ask Miss Hayley to help you find the animal puzzle'*. Now is the time to be a dynamic link between the child and the environment.

Encourage children who know the setting well to choose their own activities. You can simply invite them to leave the group and find an activity, or you can help them plan what to do next by asking them what they would like to do. If a child is a little uncertain, allow them some thinking time before stepping in with enticing suggestions: *'Ashley, why don't you go to the construction area with Toby and get out the Polydrons to play with – or would you prefer to play with the garage?'* You can also help the children to plan where in the setting to do a particular activity: *'Where would be a good place to build the fire engine floor puzzle?'* As the children disperse from the group, ask colleagues to observe how well they settle to a new activity and step in with support if necessary.

Tidying up

Ask each child to put away their chair or mat before moving on to a new activity. This encourages children to take responsibility for their physical environment. Children can also help to put away the resources you have used. Ideally, a group session should generate the possibility of a child-initiated activity linked to the group activity, and returning resources to the setting will help to make the children aware that a particular activity is available to them. If you are holding the group just before a set event such as lunchtime, make sure you finish in time for the children to help with tidying away.

CURRICULUM GUIDANCE

Finishing the group

Supporting children in making the transition from a group activity to a free choice period helps towards the following PSED stepping stone:

Show increasing independence in selecting and carrying out activities (blue ss).

Asking children to help put away chairs, mats and resources after a group helps towards the following PD stepping stone:

Show understanding of how to transport and store equipment safely (green ss).

Child participation

You will encounter many different challenges as you encourage children to participate in the group activity. Look out for the following common scenarios – how well you address them has a direct bearing on the success of the activity:

Turn-taking

Being able to wait for your turn is an important part of learning how to co-operate within a group.

Strategies

■ Avoid turn-taking games with large groups – children will tend to lose attention if they have to sit through too many turns.

■ For activities such as giving news, keep a list of the children who have contributed from day to day. This enables you to give each child a turn across a period of days, rather than trying to fit in lots of turns within one session.

■ Model appropriate behaviour by being attentive to each child. If children become restless while another child is having their turn, remind them of how you expect them to behave in the group. At the same time, don't expect the group to sit through too long a turn. Where necessary, help slower children to speed up.

■ With a small group, it is essential to offer everyone a turn. If you have children who do not want to participate, keep giving gentle encouragement but never force them.

■ Accompanying reticent children while they take their turn can offer a springboard into participating independently (see *SNAPSHOT – the reluctant turn-taker*, page 78). Observe the reluctant turn-taker throughout the day and check whether they are having general difficulties with joining in. If you feel this is the case, look into ways of helping them to adapt to the setting.

INFORMATION LINKS

For more on:

■ helping the reluctant child to participate see pages 78 and 79.

SNAPSHOT – the reluctant turn-taker

James, Conor and Manika were playing a game of animal lotto with Mrs Evans. Conor was new to the setting and still settling in. Mrs Evans asked James to have the first turn as he had played the game before. He picked a card from the bag and placed it on his lotto board. When Mrs Evans invited Conor to pick a card, he shook his head and turned away. She responded by saying gently: *'I'll take a card for you … look, Conor, it's a horse … can you find a horse on your lotto board?'* When Conor did not respond, Mrs Evans pointed to the picture of the horse, placed the card on the lotto board and said: *'Now it's Manika's turn'*. When Conor's turn came round again, he refused to pick a card, but he did point to the lotto board when asked if he could see a cat. By the end of the game, Conor was willing to take the card from Mrs Evans and place it on the lotto board without help. Over the next few weeks, Mrs Evans played lotto regularly with Conor, encouraging him to join in whenever he was willing. As he became more and more able to play independently, Mrs Evans withdrew, observing from a distance so that she could offer support if needed.

This snapshot shows the value of:

- *Gentle persistence when encouraging a child to participate.*

- *Accepting that the process will take as long as is needed.*

- *Helping the child to take his/her turn and gradually withdrawing as the child becomes able to join in independently.*

Talkative children

Some children are almost too ready to contribute to group discussion! The enthusiasm of the talkative child is delightful, and they can provide a great role model for more reticent children. However, they do sometimes need help with controlling their urge to dominate the discussion.

Strategies

- Be positive about what talkative children have to say, but at the same time, remind them that group discussion involves listening as well as talking.

- Seat talkative children next to a supporting practitioner who can encourage them to stay quiet while others have their turn.

- Activities such as news time can result in children repeating the same thing day after day. Try leading the child onto other topics with a specific question based on your knowledge of a child's recent experiences: *'Maria, tell us about the animals you saw at the zoo'*.

- Some children need help with finishing off what they are saying. Listen carefully for the right moment to step in, give a positive response and emphasize that it is now another child's turn: *'What an exciting birthday you had, Sarah. Could you tell us about your presents tomorrow because Christopher's waiting for his turn.'*

TRY THIS

Listening to children

If you have to cut off a child in full flow, make it clear that you will continue listening to their news later in the day – and be sure to carry out your promise! This technique helps to quieten talkative children, without making them feel crushed.

Reluctance to participate

Some children are reluctant to join in a group activity or contribute to a discussion.

Strategies

- Always remember that simply sitting with a group of children is a form of participation – and, for some children, this in itself is an achievement.

- Before encouraging a child to participate, establish that they have sufficiently developed language skills and physical control to sit with the other children and join in the activity.

- Once you have decided that it is appropriate to give targeted support, keep on inviting the reluctant child to contribute. Prompt them with gentle questioning and respond positively to any contribution they make, however small.

- If a child chooses not to respond, give a neutral response and move on. At all costs, avoid turning the child's reticence into an issue.

TRY THIS

Rehearsing questions

Try rehearsing a question and answer scenario, before the start of news time. Ask the child a question related to their recent experiences. When you come to ask a similar question in the group, the previous run-through will often give the child the confidence to respond. If not, at least you will have some background information to help you prompt the child.

Wandering off

It is not unusual for new or unsettled children to refuse to join a group activity or wander off once the activity has started.

Strategies

■ Consider whether the child is developmentally ready to participate in the group activity. As a broad rule of thumb, many children under three are simply not able to sit still and concentrate in a group situation.

■ Keep on including the 'wanderer' in the group, but be prepared for the process to take a while. It may take six weeks or more for the child simply to accept staying put.

■ Learning to stay in the group does not automatically mean that the child is engaging with the activity. Persist with carefully planned, age-appropriate activities and the child will gradually come to realize that group activities can be enjoyable. At the same time, language and comprehension skills will be developing, making the child better able to settle and concentrate.

■ During the process of introducing young children to group activities, ask a supporting practitioner to stay nearby, ready to occupy children who refuse to join the group or wander off.

■ If you have older children who decide to leave the group, encourage them to return and help them to settle back into the activity. Seat them next to a supporting practitioner and involve them directly in what you are doing: *'Sammi, come and show me the cat in the picture/Sammi, come and pick the next shape from the box/Sammi, come and be the baker with me when we sing "Five Currant Buns".'*

Inappropriate contributions

Occasionally, a child will express something inappropriate. This might include racist comments or a personal comment about another child in the group.

Strategies

■ A neutral response is essential, even if you find the comment offensive. Always remember that the child will simply be repeating what they have overheard from adults and older children.

■ Gently contradict the child's statement and move on. If you find certain opinions are being expressed on a regular basis, check your equal opportunities provision to see if you are doing enough to help children develop a respect for individuality and difference.

■ Sometimes, a child may say something that suggests a serious problem, such as abuse. The group activity is not the place to deal with this. Respond neutrally, make a note of the child's words and follow the procedures set out in your Child Protection policy.

WORKING WITH GROUPS OF CHILDREN

SNAPSHOT – a personal remark

A small group of children were exploring colours. The practitioner leading the activity asked Sarah if she could spot any red items in the room. One of the children in the group, Maria, had a large strawberry birth mark across one cheek. Sarah looked at Maria and said: 'Maria's face is red. Yuk, I don't like it – it's horrible.' In anticipation of possible difficulties, the practitioner had already discussed with Maria's mother how to deal with negative comments. Maria's mother had been advised that an honest explanation of her condition was the most helpful, both to Maria and the other children's developing attitudes towards difference. Following Sarah's comment, the practitioner gave Maria a warm smile and explained to the group: 'The mark on Maria's face is called a "strawberry birth mark" '. It's a very pretty colour, like a strawberry. It's called a birth mark because Maria had it on her face when she was a tiny baby.' She then smiled at Sarah and said gently, 'Maria's strawberry birthmark is not horrible, Sarah – it's just different from your face.' She paused for a moment to let her words sink in and then switched the group's attention back to the activity: 'Sarah, can you spot something green in the book corner?' Later that day, she observed Sarah stroking Maria's arm and saying 'I like strawberries.'

This snapshot shows the value of:

■ *Consulting with parents on how to help other children respond to their child's condition.*

■ *Explaining a child's condition in a positive light, rather than judging other children for making negative comments.*

Dealing with disruptions

There are a number of strategies you can use to lessen the likelihood of disruptions, and deal with them when they do occur.

Strategies

■ Planning your group activity in advance is one of the keys to avoiding disruptions. If your activity is interesting, well-rehearsed and appropriate for the age, ability level and interests of the children, you are far more likely to hold their attention.

■ Prevent many problems from occurring in the first place by having a seating plan. Make sure that certain children are seated away from each other and position children with a short attention span next to you or a supporting practitioner.

■ Give children positive reasons for sitting beside you: *'Harrison, come and keep me company'*. Eye contact and a firm, confident tone will help to avoid giving Harrison an implicit choice over sitting next to you.

■ In spite of all your carefully laid plans, disruptions are inevitable. In a large group, let the supporting practitioner sort out the disruption wherever possible. This enables you to continue concentrating on the group as a whole.

■ It takes careful judgement to decide whether to leave a disruption to the supporting practitioner or handle it yourself. As a general rule, if you have lost the attention of the whole group you will need to stop and respond (*see SNAPSHOT – a disrupted group*).

■ Always keep your standards and expectations high. Remind children of the behaviour you expect and remember that the group setting offers a good opportunity to help children explore how their actions affect others.

If a child shows continuing reluctance or difficulty over participating in a group activity, this may indicate special needs. Observe the child closely, follow the procedures in your Special Needs policy and implement an Individual Education Plan (IEP) if necessary. Some group activities may not be appropriate learning environments for certain children with special needs. Where this is the case, provide alternative learning opportunities in accordance with the child's IEP.

SNAPSHOT – a disrupted group

Richard was showing the group a book he had brought from home. Zubin's attention had wandered and he started to experiment with stamping his feet. Before the supporting practitioner could intervene, other children joined in, setting up a rhythm. By now, the attention of the group as a whole was lost. The group leader apologized to Richard for interrupting, walked across to Zubin, placed her hands on his feet and asked him to be as still as a statue. The supporting practitioner targeted other children in the group who were stamping with particular gusto, and signalled to nearby staff to come and help. Between them, the adults calmed the group. Without focusing specifically on Zubin, the group leader talked about why it is important to listen quietly when someone else is speaking. Richard was then invited to finish showing his book. During outdoor play later that day, the group leader encouraged the children to explore stamping as part of an action rhyme. She reiterated that it is fine to stamp outside, but not during a group activity.

This snapshot shows the value of:

- *Working together as a team to handle challenging behaviour.*
- *Being alert to signals from colleagues that support is needed, particularly when they are implementing a large group activity.*
- *Assessing as quickly as possible which children are at the centre of an incident and approaching them individually.*
- *Clarifying when certain behaviours are appropriate and when they are not (it's fine to stamp outdoors, but not during a group activity).*
- *Always showing courtesy to the children (the group leader apologized to Richard for interrupting him in order to respond to Zubin).*

TRY THIS

A seating plan

Put the children's name cards on chairs or sitting mats as a quick way of seating them in a particular arrangement. Ask a practitioner to help children find their names.

Spontaneous group activities

Spontaneous group activities fall into two categories – child-initiated and adult-initiated. The child-initiated group occurs when a few children spontaneously come together to explore an activity. The adult-initiated group occurs when a practitioner spots a good moment to introduce something to a small number of interested children.

Child-initiated

The child-initiated group activity is one of the best possible learning scenarios. If children form their own, spontaneous groups, you can be sure that they are interested and ready to learn. Only involve yourself if your intervention is absolutely necessary. In order to encourage and support child-initiated group activities, make sure you are doing the following:

- Enable children to be independent and do as much for themselves as possible.

- Allow good stretches of time for free choice activities.

- Organize your setting so that resources are readily available and easy for children to access.

- Provide clear floor and table space so that children can organize their own resources independently.

Adult-initiated

The spontaneous adult-initiated group activity allows you to follow up immediately on particular interests or needs. It can also be useful for giving focus to a group of children or directing their attention towards a more positive activity. Always look out for good moments to start a spontaneous group activity. Some typical triggers might include:

- Introducing colour mixing to a small group, following their discovery that yellow and blue make green.

- Naming the different parts of the sink and toilet to give focus to children lingering in the cloakroom.

- Following up the discovery of a snail in the garden by looking for more information about snails in the book corner.

Observation notes

If you are leading the group activity, you will constantly be using your observational skills to assess how the children are responding to the activity and whether you need to adjust your approach or deal with a behavioural challenge. For more in-depth observations, ask a colleague to watch from the sidelines. Without the responsibility of conducting the group, the observer will be free to focus solely on the children.

- If you are leading the group, keep gauging the children's responses to assess whether you need to speed up, slow down or change to a different activity. If you observe that they are starting to get restless, it may be time to wind up the group.

- As group leader or supporting practitioner, you need to be constantly aware of the children's emotional responses to a story or an activity. It can be impossible to predict what emotions may be triggered by an apparently innocuous story – sometimes it's the most unexpected child who gets upset or frightened.

- If you are observing from the sidelines, look out for how well the children concentrate. Body language, eye contact and facial expression will tell you the extent to which a child has engaged with the activity or discussion. How does the child respond when asked a question or given a turn? Does their response suggest that they understand what is being asked of them?

- Use observation to assess whether the group is meeting the children's needs. Is it pitched at an appropriate level? Have the children had enough previous experience to make the most of the activity? For example, do they know their letters well enough to play a letter matching lotto game? If certain children are distracted, can you see the reasons and possible solutions? For example, if they are disturbed by children playing nearby, it may help to hold future groups in a different part of the setting.

- Observe children with special needs during group activities. Is the particular group situation appropriate for them? What adjustments and/or extra provision should be made to better meet their needs?

- Observing children during group activities may contribute to the following points in the **Foundation Profile** assessment scales:
  - engaging with the activity and participating in discussion
    Dispositions and attitudes 1, 6, 7, 8, 9
    Emotional development 3, 4, 5, 6, 7, 8, 9
    Language for communication and thinking 1, 3, 4, 5, 6, 7, 8, 9
  - taking turns and co-operating with others in a group
    Social development 3, 4, 6, 7, 8, 9
  - participating in spontaneous, child-initiated group activities
    Dispositions and attitudes 1, 3, 5, 6, 7, 8, 9
    Social development 4, 5, 6, 9

> *Language for communication and thinking 2, 3, 6.*
> - For examples of observation in practice, see Snapshot on page 78.
>
> *For a summary of different observational approaches, see page 4.*

CURRICULUM GUIDANCE

Child participation

Helping children develop the ability to take turns contributes to the following PSED goal:

> *Work as part of a group or class, taking turns and sharing fairly, understanding that there need to be agreed values and codes of behaviour for groups of people, including adults and chilen, to work together harmoniously* (ELG).

Helping talkative children to make an appropriate contribution and encouraging the reluctant child to participate contributes to a number of goals, including:

> *Have a sense of belonging* (blue ss/PSED);
>
> *Initiate a conversation, negotiate positions, pay attention to and take account of others' views* (green ss/CLL);
>
> *Interact with others, negotiating plans and activities and taking turns in conversation* (ELG/CLL);
>
> *Sustain attentive listening, responding to what they have heard by relevant comments, questions or actions* (ELG/CLL).

Encouraging children to sit in a group with others and the careful handling of interruptions during group activities helps towards the following PSED goals:

> *Have an awareness of the boundaries set and behavioural expectations within the setting* (green ss);
>
> *Consider the consequences of their words and actions for themselves and others* (ELG).

Creating an environment in which spontaneous group activities can occur helps towards the following PSED stepping stones:

> *Seek out others to share experiences* (yellow ss);
>
> *Show increasing independence in selecting and carrying out activities/Show confidence in linking up with others for support and guidance* (blue ss);
>
> *Initiate interactions with other people* (green ss).

Mealtimes, using the toilet and garden play

Mealtimes, using the toilet and outdoor play are fundamental to the health and happiness of the young child. Food and toileting can be sensitive issues for some children, while going outside needs careful management if children are to gain from all that the garden has to offer.

The chapter is divided into three sections:

- Mealtimes
- Toileting
- Garden play.

Mealtimes

Nutrition is hugely important for the young child. Apart from providing healthy lunches and/or snacks, how you manage mealtimes plays an important role in helping children to develop a positive attitude towards food.

Lunchtime routines

As with any routine in the early years setting, it is important is to establish a clear system so that the children know what to expect. Your organization of mealtimes should provide the following:

- Familiar routines to help mealtimes run smoothly and give security to children who are anxious about eating.

- Opportunities to develop independence.

■ Enough time for children to eat properly, without making fast eaters wait for too long while others finish.

TRY THIS

Sharing out chores

Take photographs of children engaged in different lunchtime chores:

■ setting the table

■ pouring drinks

■ serving food.

Label each photo, laminate them and put them in a drawstring bag. Let the children pick a card to discover their lunchtime chore for that day.

TRY THIS

Pre-lunch meditations

A quiet moment before the start of the meal has many purposes:

■ establishes a sense of 'togetherness'

■ has a calming effect

■ encourages children to think beyond the 'here and now'

■ encourages children to be appreciative of their food.

Depending on the ethos of your group, you could choose an ecumenical prayer (check parents' wishes). Alternatively, ask the children to shut their eyes and say a quiet 'thank you' to whoever has prepared their delicious lunch. Encourage quietness by asking the children to listen carefully for sounds such as birdsong (remember that many children find it hard to sit still with their eyes closed).

The following routine can be adopted as it stands, or adapted to fit in with your particular setting:

■ **11.30 – laying tables:** small group of children set tables and fill cups with water/ diluted fruit juice.

■ **11.45 – washing hands:** children wash hands in small groups; supervise hand washing to ensure that it has been done thoroughly.

- **11.45 – 12.00 – sitting down:** children who are having packed lunches fetch their lunchboxes and go to their table, where staff are waiting to receive them; staff keep children occupied with conversation/finger games until the whole group is seated.

- **12.00 – quiet moment:** when everyone is settled, the group shares a 'quiet moment' (see *TRY THIS – pre-lunch meditations*, page 87).

- **12.00 onwards – eating:** children open their lunchboxes/are served their food and eat together.

- **12.30 onwards – leaving the table:** as children finish, they clear up after themselves – recycling any rubbish (food waste in the compost bin/paper in the paper bin), washing-up and wiping mats with a damp cloth. They then join an organized activity with an active component (remember that the children will have been sitting for a good 30 minutes); for example:

  - playing *What's the time Mr Wolf?*

  - using an obstacle course

  - throwing/catching sponge balls

  - playing hunt-the-thimble

  - circle dancing.

- **12.30 onwards – slow eaters:** a staff member stays with the slow eaters, helping them to finish up and clear away. When all children have finished, an adult re-washes the plates, cutlery and mats (out of sight of the children).

As with all routines, the key to success lies in careful preparation and working as a team, with everyone fulfilling their particular roles; for example:

- Ensuring that the 'table monitors' know where to find everything so that they can set the table independently.

- Preparing enough washing-up facilities so that children do not have to wait for too long to clear up after themselves.

TRY THIS

Cleaning teeth

Encourage children to take responsibility for personal hygiene by cleaning teeth after lunch. Ask parents to provide toothbrush and toothpaste in a named washbag and check that children only use a pea-sized amount of toothpaste.

- Being in place to supervise hand washing, sit with children when they come to the table or welcome children into an activity group once they have finished.

- Sharing responsibility with colleagues for checking that children are never left unsupervised at the table, in case of choking or allergic reactions.

Packed lunches

If you do not have facilities for preparing meals, children will need to bring packed lunches. Ask parents to provide lunchboxes and food containers that are designed for children and easy for them to open by themselves.

You will probably see a huge variety in the quality of packed lunches. If you are concerned about packed lunches, you can request that certain items are not brought into the setting (fizzy drinks, sweets, nuts). You can also (tactfully) offer parents some guidelines for nutritious options. Although providing the lunch is the parent's responsibility, have a quick look as the children unpack their lunch boxes. Busy parents can sometimes miss mould on bread or fruit that is on the turn (see *SNAPSHOT – checking lunchboxes*). Show parents what their children have eaten by putting any unfinished food back into the lunchbox.

SNAPSHOT – checking lunchboxes

Harriet had a thermos of soup in her lunchbox. She poured out her soup, took a mouthful and then spat it out, saying *'there's a stone in my soup'*. The staff member sitting at her table checked Harriet's cup, only to find that the thermos had broken and there were shards of glass in the soup. She helped Harriet to wash out her mouth and filled in the Accident book. Later that day, staff agreed on the following policy:

- all children should be watched closely while unpacking their lunchboxes;
- parents should be asked not to use any glass containers;
- parents should be asked only to send in thermos flasks designed for use by children.

One staff member agreed to source appropriate thermos flasks and pass on recommendations to parents.

This snapshot shows the value of:

- *Close supervision at all stages of the meal.*
- *Assessing an unfortunate incident as a team and deciding on strategies to prevent the incident from re-occurring.*
- *Giving parents up-to-date information about suitable lunchbox containers.*

You will also need to have contingency plans in case a parent forgets to send in a lunchbox. If it all possible, contact the parent so that they can bring in the forgotten lunch. If your setting does not normally provide lunches, it is preferable for parents to provide their child's packed lunch as they can accommodate any allergies, intolerances and the child's likes and dislikes. In the event of the parent being unable to bring in the lunchbox, keep a range of appropriate and safely stored foods. Double-check for allergies and special diets before offering the child an alternative to their usual packed lunch.

Prepared lunches

Prepared lunches allow you to monitor more closely what the children eat when they are in the setting. Your daily menu must provide at least one food from each of the following groups:

- carbohydrate – bread/cereals/grains/potatoes
- fruit/vegetables (cooked and raw)
- dairy foods
- meat/fish/vegetarian protein.

For example, a lunch of vegetable risotto with chicken or quorn, salad of tomatoes and cucumber, followed by bananas and custard provides:

- carbohydrate (rice)
- vegetables (cooked and raw)
- meat protein (chicken)
- vegetarian protein (quorn)
- fruit (bananas)
- dairy (custard).

Involve both parents and children in the planning of menus. Hold a parent meeting to discuss balancing good nutrition with children's likes and dislikes and help children to understand which foods they should eat at mealtimes and which foods should be saved for occasional treats. Make sure that you provide meal choices to cater for different cultural backgrounds and special diets (see page 91), and offer as much choice as possible. Provide weekly menus so that parents can tick their preferred options and offer the children daily choices; for example, would they like tomatoes and/or cucumber with their risotto? It is also important to let parents know what their child has eaten. Prepare a chart with each child's name and space to note what sized portion they ate, and whether they left any component of the meal. Have this information available for parents when they collect their child.

Involve the children in self service and serving food to others. Plan a rota giving every child a turn at serving and incorporate easy-to-serve single portions into your daily menu, such as cherry tomatoes and flapjacks. Find serving implements that the children can manage, such as a spoon and a fish slice. Where appropriate, source specialized implements for children with co-ordination difficulties and be ready to support any child who needs extra help so that they can participate in serving food.

Allergies and special diets

It is essential that parents record any allergies, intolerances or special diets on their child's registration form. A list of children with allergies and special diets should be displayed on the staff notice board, with all staff remembering to check the list on a regular basis. Make it clear to parents that you will provide for special diets and that staff will not make any child feel 'labelled' or 'singled out' due to their diet. Ask parents to provide as much written information as possible about what their child should/shouldn't eat – for example, it can be complicated to work out what is acceptable for a vegan child as animal-based ingredients are hidden in so many foods.

Occasionally, an allergy is so severe that a child cannot be in the presence of the culprit food (see *SNAPSHOT – handling severe allergies*). Check with parents the severity of any allergy and, if necessary, seek advice from your local health visitor. Ask parents to send in appropriate treats on special occasions so that the child does not miss out. Consider placing a blanket ban on nuts as these can cause such extreme allergic reactions.

SNAPSHOT – handling severe allergies

Thomas was sitting next to Asher at the lunch table. Miss Alice was supervising the table and noticed both boys laughing as Asher tapped Thomas's face. Suddenly, Thomas complained that his eye felt hot and sore. Knowing that he had an allergy to eggs, Alice checked Asher's lunch and discovered that his fingers were covered in egg from his sandwich. She followed appropriate procedures for dealing with Thomas's allergic reaction and later discussed the event with his father. His father confirmed that Thomas reacted to skin contact with egg. Alice added this to Thomas's record, told her colleagues and posted a notice on the staff board informing everyone that Thomas must not sit near anyone with eggs in their lunchbox.

This snapshot shows the value of:

■ *Keeping a constant look out for choking and allergic reactions at the lunch table.*

■ *Gathering as much information as possible from parents about an allergy or special diet.*

■ *Remembering to update all colleagues when the setting receives new information about a child with an allergy or special diet.*

Fussy and reluctant eaters

Fussy eating can cause a huge amount of parental anxiety. As a professional childcare worker, you can play a major role in helping reluctant eaters to develop a more positive attitude towards food.

Strategies

■ Find out how parents approach their child's eating difficulties and the role they would like you to play. Suggest that you use gentle persistence and keep on encouraging the child to have a little taste. Research shows that it takes several tastes to become used to a new food, so it is worth persisting – even if the child is only managing two peas at a time!

■ Emphasize to the parents that you will avoid pressurizing the child or adding to their anxieties about food. Discuss the importance of adopting a relaxed approach and keeping mealtimes enjoyable (often easier for you to achieve than the parents).

■ Use your judgement over what it is reasonable for a child to eat. If a parent puts the child's entire five fruit portions in their lunchbox, you will probably fail in getting the child to finish them!

■ If a child usually has a balanced diet, do not force them to eat foods that they genuinely dislike.

■ Sometimes, children develop a fear of food. Where this is the case, encourage them to explore food without having to taste it. Save leftover fruit from snack time and let the child feel and sniff them. Use porridge for 'messy play' and real pastry for model making.

■ If you need specific advice on eating difficulties, contact your local health visitor and encourage parents to do the same.

TRY THIS

Using picture books

Vivian French's *Oliver's Fruit Salad* (Hodder Children's Books) is a great way to explore healthy eating, particularly with children who do not like fruit and vegetables.

Table 'rules' and lunchtime conversations

Sharing a meal is an enjoyable social occasion and one that many children do not experience at home. As with all social events, children gain far more if they understand how to conduct themselves appropriately. While this does not have to mean a return to Victorian table manners, a few guidelines will support the children as they learn to manage food, cutlery and mealtime conversation. Involve the children in planning the 'rules' and emphasize what they should be doing, rather than what they shouldn't. For example:

■ Ask politely if you want someone to pass you something (do some practice role plays).

■ Empty your mouth before you speak.

- Try to make your crumbs fall onto your plate.

- Any food dropped on the floor should not be eaten but thrown in the recycling bin.

- Eat savoury foods before sweet foods (savoury foods tend to be more nutritious).

- Stay in your seat until washing-up time.

- Do not swap lunchbox food (be firm about this – someone else's food may not be appropriate or safe for a particular child).

Introduce appropriate cutlery, such as knives and forks or chopsticks, when children have developed sufficient dexterity to manage them (see *TRY THIS – using cutlery*). At the same time, be sensitive and accommodating to children who come from cultural backgrounds where food is eaten with the fingers. Encourage all children to feed themselves and organize their food as independently as possible; for example, if a child is struggling to peel a banana, open it for them and then let them finish it off.

Apart from the food, conversation is what makes a mealtime a pleasant occasion. Food makes a great discussion topic – talk about the names, shapes, colours and tastes of different foods; look at the writing and pictures on packets and discuss where a particular food originates; can children decide which part of the plant a particular vegetable comes from, or find the seeds in a banana?

TRY THIS

Using cutlery

Explore cutlery through play. Scoop up sand with a spoon. Use real knives, forks and serving implements with playdough and clay. Introduce chopsticks to the home corner. Demonstrate the correct way to use the cutlery, although the emphasis should be on enjoying the different implements and becoming familiar with them.

Snacks

Snacks are an important source of nutrition and energy for young children. Fruit and vegetable chunks make a colourful snack and will help you meet your target for providing raw vegetables (with their greater vitamin/mineral content). Try carrot circles, cherry tomatoes, cucumber sticks, kiwi slices and apple boats. Seedless grapes are popular, but they should be cut in half to avoid the risk of choking. You should also offer milk and water. If children are reluctant to take these drinks, you can give diluted fruit juice (one part juice/five parts water) with a snack or meal. Drinking juice with food lessens its impact on teeth, but it should not be freely available throughout the day. For more snack suggestions, see *SNAPSHOT – free access to snacks* and *TRY THIS – a snack table*, page 94.

SNAPSHOT – free access to snacks

Staff had noticed that several children were becoming either listless or over-boisterous as the morning progressed. Eventually, the setting manager sought advice from her health visitor, who asked whether the children were getting a good breakfast before they arrived in the morning, whether water was freely available and at what time they had a snack. When the setting manager explained that the children were given milk and a biscuit at 10.30, the health visitor pointed out that some children could be going for a very long period without sustenance and that low blood sugar might be the cause of the behavioural issues. She suggested making water, fruit and vegetable chunks freely available throughout the morning, with staff encouraging children who displayed negative behaviours to snack and drink. She also suggested a protein based snack at 10.30 (cheese, ham or hummous with an oatcake). The staff implemented her suggestions (see *TRY THIS — a snack table*) and noticed an immediate improvement in behaviour.

This snapshot shows the value of:

■ *Exploring the underlying reasons for negative behaviour patterns.*

■ *Seeking specialist advice when necessary.*

■ *Providing children with free access to healthy drinks and snacks.*

TRY THIS

A snack table

Cover a table with an attractive cloth and set out two or three chairs. Provide covered jugs of water and milk, cups, a platter of fruit and vegetable chunks and washing-up facilities. Explain to the children that they can use the snack table whenever they wish and practise pouring drinks and washing up cups. Keep an eye on the snack table to make sure it is being used appropriately. Encourage all children to snack at some point in the morning and gently discourage any children who snack too much. Make sure that milk is not left out for too long, particularly during hot weather.

 # Observation notes

Targeted observations at snack and lunchtime will tell you about a child's attitude to food, how well they cope with mealtime routines and whether your mealtime routines need modification to make them more manageable for the children.

■ Use your lunchtime observations as the basis for deciding whether a child is ready to try using cutlery. If you observe that a child is having difficulty opening their lunchbox, consider asking the parents to provide something more manageable when they are next replacing the lunchbox.

■ Observe how well the children conduct themselves at the table and eat their food. Do you need to reiterate any 'table rules' or encourage children to eat a bit more of their lunch?

■ Observe how children manage mealtime routines such as washing-up. Look out for any possible problem areas and make changes if necessary. For example, if children have difficulty stacking their plates in the drying rack, try to find a rack that is easier for them to use.

■ If you provide a snack table with free access to snacks and drinks, observe closely to ensure that the table is used properly. Based on your observations, encourage any 'reluctant snackers' to use the table.

■ Observe children with special needs during snack and mealtimes. How well do they cope with their food? Are there any strategies you need to put in place to give additional support?

■ Observing how children manage food and mealtimes may contribute to the following points in the **Foundation Profile** assessment scales:

- *Physical development 5, 6, 7, 8, 9.*

■ For examples of mealtime observation in action, see Snapshots on pages 89, 91 and 94.

For a summary of different observational approaches, see page 4.

Nap time

Many children will need a nap, particularly if they stay for a full day. Provide a quiet area with wipeable mats, pillows, blankets and cuddly toys so that children can rest if they wish to. This area should be freely available to children throughout the day and the group need to understand that it is a rest area and not for playing. The rest area should also be located so that it is away from any main thoroughfare in the setting – apart from the need for quiet, it is essential that sleeping children aren't stepped on or tripped over! You should also pay particular attention to hygiene; clean mats with antibacterial wipes and wash bedding regularly.

If children are not tired, don't force them to rest. Rather than timetabling a rest period, watch out for children who seem to be flagging (particularly after lunch) and encourage them to use the rest area. Watch out also for those children who express tiredness by becoming more and more boisterous. Offer a calming activity such as letting children lie down while you put on a CD. The ones who are really tired will fall asleep, even if there is a story to listen to.

CURRICULUM GUIDANCE

Mealtimes/naps

Learning how to behave appropriately at the table and the social element of mealtimes helps towards a number of PSED goals, including:

> *Form good relationships with adults and peers* (ELG);
>
> *Have an awareness of the boundaries set and behavioural expectations within the setting* (green ss);
>
> *Consider the consequences of their words and actions for themselves and others* (ELG).

Mealtimes offer lots of opportunities for language development; for example, asking for what you need and table conversation. This helps towards a number of CLL goals, including:

> *Talk alongside others, rather than with them. Use talk to gain attention and initiate exchanges...* (green ss);
>
> *Speak clearly and audibly with confidence and control and show awareness of the listener, for example by their use of conventions such as greetings, 'please' and 'thank you'* (ELG).

Managing lunchboxes and/or cutlery, setting the table and doing the washing-up helps towards a number of PD goals, including:

> *Use one-handed tools and equipment* (yellow ss);
>
> *Handle tools, objects, construction and malleable materials safely and with increasing control* (ELG).

Helping children develop healthy eating patterns, realize the importance of hygiene at mealtimes and the need to rest helps towards a number of PD goals, including:

> *Show awareness of own needs with regard to eating, sleeping and hygiene* (yellow ss);
>
> *Show some understanding that good practices with regard to exercise, eating, sleeping and hygiene can contribute to good health* (green ss);
>
> *Recognize the importance of keeping healthy and those things which contribute to this* (ELG).

Toileting

Using the toilet is a common source of anxiety for many young children, particularly when they are not in their home surroundings. If children are given a familiar and manageable routine to follow, they are far more likely to use the toilet successfully.

Toilet routines

Organize toilets and wash basins so that children can use them independently. Ideally, toilets should be small scale, but if you have a setting with adult-sized toilets, provide sturdy non-slip stools. If the toilet has an overhead cistern, check that the children can reach the chain and add extra chain if necessary. Remove any locks, although it is preferable to have doors for those children who prefer privacy (see *SNAPSHOT – toilet privacy*, page 99).

Check daily that your hot tap is set at an appropriate temperature. If possible, remove plugs from the sink – if a child uses the plug and then forgets to turn off the tap, you can end up with a flood. Provide disposable paper towels or an electric hand dryer. If you wish to use fabric towels and flannels, each child should have their own named towel and flannel and they should be washed daily.

Introducing toilet routines should be one of your priorities when children first start at the setting. Show them techniques such as:

- How to tear off or pull out just two or three pieces of toilet paper and wrap them around the hand.

- Putting up the seat (for older boys who stand to use the toilet).

- Wiping the toilet seat with a fresh piece of paper.

- Flushing the toilet.

TRY THIS

Aiming straight

If you have older boys who stand up to use the toilet, try this technique to help them improve their aim:

- Place your hand gently in the small of the child's back and encourage him to arch his back a little – this puts the child in a better position to aim accurately.

- Challenge him to 'hit the water' in the toilet and see if he can manage not to wet the toilet seat or floor.

After children have finished using the toilet, it is essential that they wash their hands. Break the process of hand washing into single stages and demonstrate each stage:

- Pulling up sleeves.

- Turning on the tap.

- Wetting hands.

- Lathering the soap.

- Soaping hands from finger tips to wrist.

- Rinsing hands thoroughly (show children how to check that all the lather has gone).

- Taking just one paper towel/finding their own towel/turning on the hand dryer and drying hands.

- Throwing the paper towel in the bin/replacing the fabric towel/turning off the hand dryer.

Focus on *showing* the children what to do – for example, a demonstration of how to lather the soap will be much more effective than an explanation. You should also help the children to understand the reasons for these different activities. Why might it be necessary to wipe the seat? Why is it important to wash your hands? Children who understand why they are following through a particular routine are much more likely to remember what to do.

TRY THIS

Washing hands routine

Take photographs of a child coming out of the toilet, turning on the tap, wetting hands and so on. Add written captions, laminate the photographs and display them in sequence in the toilet to remind the children of the washing hands process.

TRY THIS

Using picture books

Tony Ross's *Little Princess Books* are a fun way of exploring sensitive issues with children. Try *Wash Your Hands* and *I Want My Potty!* (both published by Kane/Miller).

SNAPSHOT – toilet privacy

Staff at four-year-old Hannah's setting had a routine of taking children to the toilets in groups, before play time and lunch. Although Hannah had always been happy to use the toilet, she was starting to show reluctance and having the odd accident. Staff discussed the situation with Hannah's mother and asked whether an upset at home or nursery was causing her to regress. Hannah's mother was unable to think of anything and decided to ask Hannah about the toilets at nursery. Hannah complained that she didn't need to go when the teachers said she had to and she didn't like everyone looking at her when she sat on the toilet. The mother reported Hannah's comments back to the staff. They agreed that Hannah should be allowed to skip the 'group' toilet sessions and encouraged to use the toilet independently. Hannah adjusted happily to this new routine and her accidents ceased.

This snapshot shows the value of:

- *Consulting with both parents and child when trying to find the reasons for a child's distress.*
- *Being flexible over group routines to suit the needs of the individual child.*
- *Enabling children to use the toilets as independently as possible.*

Toilet training

Some settings will only accept children who are fully toilet trained. Bear in mind that you may be in breach of legislation regarding inclusion if you refuse to take a child whose toileting difficulties are caused by a disability. By far the best approach is to welcome all children, regardless of where they are at with toileting, and work with them and their parents to help them progress to the next stage. The 'normal' stages in toileting for the three-plus age group are:

- **2 to 3 years:** children become aware that they need the toilet and can hold on for a short time if necessary. They can indicate that they want the toilet though words and/or gestures.

- **3 to 4 years:** children become more reliable in asking to use the toilet, although accidents still happen.

- **4 to 5 years:** children become fully independent in using the toilet and are mostly dry at night. Accidents may still happen if a child is tired, upset or unwell.

Of course, many children fall outside this pattern. If a three year old is still in nappies when they start at your setting, agree on a strategy with the child's parents so that both home and school are following a similar routine. If toileting issues are the result of special needs, make it absolutely clear to parents that you are happy to do whatever is necessary to support the child and their particular toileting needs. Let the parents take the lead and be vigilant so that any problems can be resolved swiftly. (Many parents have a tale to tell about how their child's toilet difficulties began with an incident at nursery!)

When planning a routine with parents, consider the following:

■ Agree that both parents and setting will use the same approach to toileting.

■ Check whether the child is happier on a potty or a toilet. Would a toilet booster seat be helpful?

■ Discuss steps to help the child adjust to the toilet or potty, such as:

  – watching others use the toilet (remember that some children prefer privacy – see *SNAPSHOT – toilet privacy*, page 99);

  – sitting on the toilet fully clothed;

  – sitting on the toilet wearing a nappy with a hole cut in it (this enables the child to use the toilet while retaining the security of the nappy pad).

■ Do parents have any religious or cultural wishes that you need to be aware of?

■ What signs or words does the child use to indicate that he or she needs the toilet?

■ Emphasize the importance of dressing the child in clothes that can be pulled down quickly.

■ Reassure parents that you have nappy changing facilities and explain your nappy changing policy (see page 101).

■ Reassure parents that no child will ever be made to feel anxious about toileting, and that you will handle the process with patience and good humour.

■ Try to avoid making parents feel pressured or judged over their child's toilet training. Toileting can be a source of great anxiety and everyone will benefit if you are able to help parents feel more relaxed about the whole process.

TRY THIS

No pull ups

Suggest to parents that they do not send their children in pull up nappies. The discomfort of wet pants helps children to realize that they have wet themselves, giving them an incentive to use the toilet. Reassure parents that you are happy to change children if there are any accidents.

INFORMATION LINKS
For more detailed information on: ■ toilet training, including toileting for children with special needs see Further Reading.

Managing the toilet

There are various little techniques you can use to help children manage the toilet and support children who are still going through the toilet training process.

Strategies

- Look out for signs that a child needs the toilet – pulling at clothes, wriggling, stepping from side to side. Always respond by taking the child to the toilet.

- Make sure that children know how to ask for the toilet. Establish the signs or wording used by children in the home or agree on simple wording such as 'toilet please' and practise asking to go to the toilet as a role play activity.

- Even if you take groups of children to the toilet at set times, encourage children to go whenever they want and designate a staff member to keep an eye on the toilets.

- Never make children feel rushed when using the toilet.

- Give lots of praise for using the toilet and washing hands. Tailor your praise to suit whatever stage the child has reached – for some, it might simply be asking to go, for others, it could be rinsing out the wash basin or helping another child.

- Be patient about accidents. They are inevitable, particularly at the start of the year. Try to respond efficiently and in a calm and neutral manner.

TRY THIS

Mop and bucket

Have a mop and bucket of hot water and disinfectant ready to use at all times. This will help you deal with accidents quickly and hygienically. Make sure the bucket is kept safely out of the children's reach.

Nappy changing

All settings should provide a nappy changing area for children who are not toilet trained. Not all staff in Foundation stage settings are comfortable with changing nappies and nappy changing should ideally be voluntary, with just a couple of staff members taking on the responsibility. Discuss nappy changing with new staff and include toileting responsibilities in their job descriptions.

Nappy changing should take place in a room separate from the main setting. It should be warm and private, with a changing mat, hypoallergenic wipes, disinfectant wipes and disposable gloves. Soiled nappies should be placed immediately in nappy bags and disposed of properly (incinerated or collected for disposal).

CURRICULUM GUIDANCE

Toileting

Learning how to use the toilet and wash hands is an important part of managing bodily functions and personal hygiene, contributing to the following PD goals:

Show awareness of own needs with regard to eating, sleeping and hygiene (yellow ss);

Show awareness of a range of healthy practices with regard to eating, sleeping and hygiene (blue ss);

Show some understanding that good practices with regard to exercise, eating, sleeping and hygiene can contribute to good health (green ss);

Recognize the importance of keeping healthy and those things which contribute to this (ELG).

Garden play

Going outside gives children fresh air and sunlight, the chance to shout, run around and explore nature. Whether you have the luxury of a large, landscaped garden or are simply making the most of a small courtyard, your outdoor provision is just as important as your indoor setting.

Preparing the outdoor environment

When planning your outdoor environment, remember that you should be catering for all six Areas of Learning, just as you do indoors. Store resources in wheeled cabinets so that they can easily be taken outdoors and choose resources that link with the outdoor environment; for example:

- Make up an outdoor dressing-up box with appropriate outfits such as firefighters and construction workers.

- Put scarves, shawls and headdresses in with a box of percussion instruments to encourage outdoor music and dance performances.

■ Gather a selection of 'outdoor' books with subject matter such as weather, nature and garden play.

■ Make up a box of natural items such as fir cones, pebbles, feathers and twigs. Encourage children to use them for imaginative play, pattern making and counting.

■ Provide equipment so that children can care for the outdoor environment; for example, brooms, rakes and wheelbarrows.

■ Provide equipment to help children explore the garden; for example, magnifying glasses and binoculars (carefully supervised), bug bottles, a flower press and notebooks for recording discoveries.

Wherever possible, set up an 'outdoor version' of your indoor resources; for example:

■ washing lines for displays

■ outdoor blackboards

■ 'water' painting (painting areas such as fences and tarmac with water and decorating brushes)

■ an 'activity circle' made from slices of wood for spontaneous and planned group activities

■ materials such as planks of wood, old curtains and pegs for building dens and other large-scale constructions

■ large sheets of garden netting for threading and weaving

■ a gardening area.

You will also need to plan the garden area to offer a range of facilities and areas; for example:

■ different surfaces (grass, tarmac, cobbles...)

■ ground markings such as hopscotch grids

■ shady areas with seating (trees, pagodas, parasols)

■ a 'wild' area

■ climbing equipment, slides and swings

■ areas for sand and water play

■ outdoor play settings (Wendy house, building site, road system with zebra crossing)

■ 'landscaping' such as ramps, low walls, steps, slopes and tunnels

■ appropriate provision and access for children with disabilities and special needs.

TRY THIS

Garden chores and rotas

- Take photographs of different garden chores such as raking leaves or gathering up toys. Show whose turn it is to do outdoor chores by pegging the photographs on the washing line, alongside a child's name card.

- Make a rota for popular equipment by pegging up name cards alongside a picture of the equipment.

Getting ready to go outside

Going outside needs careful preparation, particularly when the children have to put on outdoor clothes or suncream. As with all routines, encourage children to do as much for themselves as possible (see *TRY THIS – putting on coats*, page 61). Start off a zip and let the child finish pulling it up; show children how to manage their buttons; get them to put on boots before coats so they are not hampered by bulky sleeves. Most children enjoy the challenge and achievement of getting themselves ready, although you do need to check that coats have been done up and hats and gloves put on if the weather is cold.

Suncare

Sun safety has become an increasingly important issue over the last few years and you need to ensure that children are properly protected when they go outside.

Strategies

- Ask parents to provide suncream (minimum factor 15), sunglasses and a wide brimmed sunhat (baseball caps do not protect the neck).

- Use suncream liberally and don't forget the neck, ears, cheeks, nose, arms, hands and feet. Re-apply regularly, particularly after water play.

- In very hot weather, ask parents to dress their children in closely woven material such as t-shirts.

- Limit the time spent in the sun. Make the most of shady areas and be particularly careful between 11am and 3pm when the sun is at its strongest.

- Remember that children can still burn on cloudy/breezy days.

- Make sure the children drink regularly. If you have reluctant water drinkers, provide heavily diluted juice and lots of fruit snacks.

- Plan for the time it will take to get children ready for outdoor play in the sun.

Free garden access

Free access to the garden is something that more and more settings are aiming to provide. 'Free access' means enabling children to go outside whenever they choose. Although it takes a bit of planning, the advantages are enormous:

- Children are able to 'let off steam' whenever they wish.

- Children are able to move more vigorously than most indoor environments can accommodate.

- Free access increases the opportunity for children to develop gross motor movements and discover their physical capabilities and limits.

- A carefully planned garden allows children more privacy and peace than many indoor environments.

- Children can engage in an outdoor activity for as long as they wish, without being interrupted because playtime has ended.

- A well-supervised outdoor setting can be less stressful for children who have difficulty with physical and/or emotional self control.

- In a society where children are increasingly kept indoors, free garden access allows them to get plenty of fresh air and sunlight.

When planning the provision of free garden access, you need to take into consideration the following:

- **The Areas of Learning:** if children are spending a lot of time outside, you must make comprehensive outdoor provision for the six Areas of Learning.

- **Getting ready:** explain the importance of getting ready to go outside and help children learn how to manage outdoor clothes as independently as possible. Keep a constant eye on the cloakroom to give reminders, offer help and apply suncream where necessary. If you are the staff member supervising outdoors, check that the children are wearing coats, sunhats and so on as they come outside.

- **Weather protection:** ask parents to provide appropriate outdoor clothing, including waterproofs for rainy weather. Provide pergolas, parasols and water tight play houses to protect against sun and rain. Earmark old towels for drying seats and show the children how to crawl into washable sleeping bags during cold weather. As long as children are properly dressed, they can go out in just about any weather (although you may need to set limits during downpours and excessively hot or cold days).

- **Supervision:** all parts of the garden need to be constantly supervised. Set up a rota to ensure that there are always staff outside (see *Safety, Supervision* pages 106–7 and *Garden rules*, pages 107–8).

■ **'Indoor' children:** be aware of those children who choose to stay indoors and encourage them to go outside for exercise, fresh air and a change of scene. Wherever possible, hold planned activities outdoors.

Safety and supervision

Safety and supervision are particularly important in the garden. Vigorous outdoor activities can lead to accidents and if you have a multiple-use setting, such as a church hall, your outdoor area needs to be checked carefully for litter.

When planning your garden setting, bear in mind the following:-

■ remove poisonous/thorny plants

■ cut back bushes with sharp twigs

■ check that gates and fencing are secure

■ fence off/cover garden ponds

■ lock up garden implements

■ check for uneven paving slabs

■ check that playground equipment complies with European safety standards before purchase

■ lay an impact absorbing surface (not grass) beneath any equipment where children stand at a height of above 6cm off the ground.

Do a thorough daily check of the outdoor setting, looking out for:

■ broken glass

■ litter

■ animal mess (particularly in soil or sand)

■ holes in fences

■ unsecured gates

■ clean sand in sandpit

■ pools of water on seats/equipment

■ ice patches (sprinkle with sand)

■ boggy lawns / flooded areas.

Large equipment should have a safety check once a term, although you should keep a constant eye on all outdoor resources to make sure they are in good working order.

Apart from setting up a safe environment, all parts of your outdoor area should be supervised at all times. Do a survey of the garden and work out where different adults need to be 'posted' (don't forget hidden areas – see *SNAPSHOT – supervising outdoor play*, page 108). Double-check that you know where to stand and which part of the garden is your responsibility. Aim to be on a constant state of 'high alert' and try not to be distracted by chatting to other adults. There should also be roving staff who can deal with any incidents that arise and play with the children. However, although close supervision is important, bear in mind that space and freedom are part of what makes garden play so valuable. Try to avoid over-organizing the children, or preventing them from exploring possibilities. Although safety is essential, children who are over-protected will not discover their limits or learn to recognize the difference between a genuine hazard and an activity that is perfectly safe if approached sensibly.

TRY THIS

A garden checklist

Prepare a photocopiable checklist for your garden, including 'litter', 'broken glass', 'wet seats' and so on. Design the list so that the checker can put in the date and tick off each item to show that the garden has been checked for that day.

Garden rules

As part of providing a safe, stimulating and well-supervised outdoor setting, it is useful to have some guidelines for both adults and children. Discuss garden play with the children and ask them to help you decide on a set of 'rules'. Although these will vary depending on the nature of your outdoor setting, the following points are common to many settings:

- Learn the difference between rough games that hurt others and games that are simply boisterous (use role play and stories to explore this difference).

- Wait until it is your turn to play on the climbing frame (see *TRY THIS – garden chores and rotas*, page 104, for a way of setting up a rota for popular equipment).

- Use brakes or feet when playing with wheeled toys. (Remind children that Mummy doesn't crash into other people when she drives the car!)

- Avoid walking in front of/behind the swings.

- Check with an adult before picking flowers or leaves (if possible, provide a wild area and let children pick common lawn flowers such as daisies).

- Tell an adult if you find something dangerous such as:

  - glass

  - litter

  - broken toys

- Put away all garden toys after you have finished with them.

- Try not to disturb children who want to sit quietly in shady areas.

SNAPSHOT – supervising outdoor play

It was a sunny day and lots of the children were playing outside in the garden. Shona came up to Mrs Lewis to tell her that James had bitten her arm in the Wendy house. As she seemed unconcerned, Mrs Lewis suggested that she join her other friends under the tree. The next morning, Shona's mother showed the setting manager a bite mark on Shona's arm and demanded to know why she hadn't been informed when she collected her daughter. The setting manager promised to investigate the incident and, at a meeting later that day, staff agreed to survey the garden and make a note of all 'hidden areas'. It was also agreed that staff would check for possible injuries following every incident, however minor the incident appeared to be. The setting manager informed Shona's mother of the action the setting would be taking to prevent such an incident from happening again.

This snapshot shows the value of:

- *Supervising every part of the outdoor setting, including the 'hidden areas'.*

- *Assessing an incident and agreeing as a team on strategies to prevent a recurrence of the incident.*

- *Informing parents of the strategies you have set in place, following an incident involving their child.*

CURRICULUM GUIDANCE

Garden play

Outdoor activities and using garden toys and equipment play an important part in many PD goals, including:

Travel around, under, over and through balancing and climbing equipment (ELG);

Operate equipment by means of pulling and pushing movements (yellow ss);

Construct with large materials such as cartons, long lengths of fabric and planks (blue ss);

Show increasing control in using equipment for climbing, scrambling, sliding and swinging (blue ss);

Use increasing control over an object by touching, pushing, patting, throwing, catching or kicking it (green ss).

Playing safely in the garden and being aware of others contributes to many PD goals, including:

Understand that equipment and tools have to be used safely (blue ss);

Handle tools, objects, construction and malleable materials safely and with increasing control (ELG).

Active garden play helps children become aware of the role of exercise in their lives, contributing to the following PD goals:

Show some understanding that good practices with regard to exercise, eating, sleeping and hygiene can contribute to good health (green ss);

Recognize the importance of keeping healthy and those things which contribute to this (ELG);

Recognize the changes that happen to their bodies when they are active (ELG).

Exploring the outdoor environment helps children to learn about their environment. This contributes to a number of KUW goals, including:

Examine objects and living things to find out more about them (green ss);

Find out about, and identify, some features of living things, objects and events they observe (ELG).

Observation notes

In many respects, outdoor observation is similar to indoor observation. There are, however, a few additional elements to look out for:

- You will often see different behaviours and characteristics emerge in the more relaxed environment of the garden. Look out for how the children interact with each other, who emerges as a leader and how well they organize their games and co-operative play.

- Garden play gives children a good opportunity to explore a range of large-scale movements such as running, jumping and sliding. Use observation to establish each child's level of physical development, who needs support and who needs to be challenged further. Look out also for children who tend to be inactive and find ways of encouraging them to participate in some physical activities.

- Observe children with special needs. Assess how well they cope with the outdoor environment and whether you need to adapt any of your facilities and/or offer additional support to help them make the most of the garden. Look out for any signs that may indicate a child with special needs such as dyspraxia (for information on dyspraxia and other special needs, see Further Reading).

- Garden play gives children a good opportunity to discover how their actions and behaviour affect others. Observe the children to establish how aware they are of safety, and whether you need to intervene and/or talk about appropriate outdoor behaviour.

- Observe different areas of the garden to see how well they are used. Extend activities that the children enjoy and look at ways of making an unpopular activity more enticing.

- Track an individual child in the garden, just as you would indoors. The child who is withdrawn or the child who does not appear to settle to anything can behave quite differently outside.

- Observing children during outdoor play may contribute to the following points in the **Foundation Profile** assessment scales:

  - the child's use of space and large-scale movements

    Physical development 1, 2, 3, 4, 6, 9

  - the child's awareness of exercise as a part of keeping healthy

    Physical development 8

  - the child's awareness of safety and how their actions affect others

    Emotional development 7, 8.

For a summary of different observational approaches, see page 4.

Supporting behaviour and relationships

One minute you're handling a temper tantrum, the next you're arbitrating in a dispute or nurturing a fledgling friendship. Sometimes, it feels as though you have to be a judge, a diplomat and a psychologist, all rolled into one! Supporting behaviour and relationships is possibly the most important, and the most challenging, aspect of the early years practitioner's role.

The chapter is divided into three sections:

■ Behaviour and social relationships

■ The child in the physical setting

■ The adult's role.

Behaviour and social relationships

When supporting relationships and responding to behavioural challenges, there are certain strategies that can be applied to any situation:

■ Agree as a team on strategies for supporting behaviour and be consistent in implementing those strategies.

■ If a problem is serious, try to deal with it away from the main part of the setting. This protects the child's privacy and helps to prevent a child getting a label amongst other children (and parents).

■ Pick and choose what to address. Sometimes you have to make a judgement that a situation is minor and needs 'nipping in the bud'. For example, if a child starts distracting their neighbour during a group activity, respond by simply placing the child's hands in their lap and continuing swiftly with the activity. On this occasion, keeping things going is more important than interrupting the whole group to discuss why we shouldn't disturb others.

■ Always give children your reasons for intervening. Explain why their behaviour is unacceptable and make sure your explanation is simple and age-appropriate – *'The children in the book corner can't hear their story if you bang your car on the floor, Christopher.'*

■ Talk about what the children *can* and *should* do rather than telling them what they shouldn't do. For example, instead of telling children not to stamp when they walk (which can be dispiriting), give them a positive challenge to strive for: *'Can you show me how quietly your feet can walk…?'* (see also *SNAPSHOT – quiet voices*).

SNAPSHOT – quiet voices

A student was observing three-year-old Sarita as she sat at a table, threading beads and singing loudly to herself. One of the practitioners came across to Sarita, leant over her and said firmly, *'Sarita is too noisy. Talk quietly, please!'* The student noticed that Sarita looked upset and although she sat quietly, she did not finish her threading. Later that day, the student observed Sarita playing in the home corner. Once again, her voice was rather loud. Her key worker came across, knelt down in front of her and said gently: *'Sarita, let me hear your quiet voice'.* Sarita smiled, put her finger on her lips and started to speak much more quietly. The student noted how much better Sarita responded to this more positive approach.

This snapshot shows the value of:

■ *Challenging a child to come up with the desired behaviour ('let me hear your quiet voice…') rather than simply telling the child what not to do and attaching negative labels ('Sarita is too noisy. Talk quietly, please!').*

■ *Careful observation following a sensitive incident, to check how the child has been affected.*

■ Wherever possible, try to re-direct negative energy towards positive activity with an enticing toy or game (see *SNAPSHOT – supporting a colleague*, page 131).

■ If family values and practices are different from those in your setting, try to avoid undermining the home. Make your expectations clear (*'**in nursery** we put away our books/say thank you/speak quietly'*) but do not make negative comments about what happens at home.

■ Give praise for appropriate behaviour – and don't forget to praise children who try, even if they don't quite manage what you were hoping for!

The following scenarios explore some of the more specific relationship and behavioural challenges you may encounter:

Nurturing friendships

Although you cannot force children to make friends, you can help them to overcome friendship difficulties and create the kind of environment where friendships can evolve.

Strategies

■ Remember that the nature of children's friendships will vary, depending on age and personality. Under-three's often 'play in parallel', operating *alongside* other children rather than *with* them. If this causes parental anxiety, explain that the child will become more aware of others and develop their ability to form co-operative relationships as they grow older.

■ Give established children some responsibility for new and/or younger children and talk about the group as 'all friends together'. At the same time, recognize that many children like to play with and sit next to special friends.

■ Try not to organize the children's every moment. Give them the time and space to socialize. Ensure that there are free choice periods throughout the day and let them choose who to play with.

■ If a child is isolated, it may be because they don't know how to approach others. Model the 'joining in' process and keep on persisting if it takes a while for them to integrate (see *SNAPSHOT – joining in*).

INFORMATION LINKS

For more on:

■ established children supporting new children see pages 11–12 and 20.

SNAPSHOT – joining in

Harriet's key worker had observed that she was not joining in with the other children and he decided it was time to offer some support. He said to her: '*Harriet, shall we go and ask James and Rashid if you can join in their game?*' Harriet nodded and held out her hand. The key worker led her to James' and Rashid's table and asked:

'*Boys, can Harriet join in your game?*'

'*But we've already started,*' said James.

'*That's all right, James*', said the key worker, '*we'll ask Emma if Harriet can play with her.*'

SNAPSHOT – continued

The key worker led Harriet to Emma's table and repeated his question:

'Emma, can Harriet join in your game?'

'OK,' replied Emma, *'here's some puzzle pieces, Harriet.'*

The key worker observed Harriet regularly and continued modelling how to join in whenever she seemed to be having difficulty. By the end of term, he was able to record that Harriet was starting to join in without support.

This snapshot shows the value of:

- *Observing the isolated child so that you can offer support over joining in when needed.*
- *Modelling how to join in with others.*
- *Persisting until you find children who are happy for a reticent child to join in, and never forcing children to play together ('that's all right James … we'll ask Emma').*

TRY THIS

Positive actions

'Being kind', 'sharing' and 'helping' are abstract concepts for young children. Illustrate their meaning by displaying photos of children engaged in positive activities. For example:

- sharing a toy
- setting the table
- pouring a drink for a younger child
- comforting a crying friend.

Write a caption for each picture (*'we are kind to our friends'/'we help with lunch'*). Refer to the pictures whenever you are discussing feelings and behaviours.

CURRICULUM GUIDANCE

Nurturing friendships

Supporting friendships helps towards many PSED goals:-

Have a sense of belonging (blue ss);

Initiate interactions with other people (green ss);

Seek out others to share experiences / Relate and make attachments to other members of the group (yellow ss);

Form good relationships with adults and peers (ELG).

Disagreements and sharing

At this young age, children often clash when they both want the same toy or are frustrated at having to wait their turn. Dealing with lots of disagreements can become wearing, particularly if you didn't witness what happened. The following strategies may come in useful.

Strategies

■ Stand back and let the children sort out a dispute by themselves. Only step in if the disagreement escalates beyond their control.

■ If you didn't witness the start of a disagreement, you cannot know who is 'in the right'. In this instance, simply make the fairest judgement you can. Be kind but firm and ensure that any solutions are carried through (see *SNAPSHOT – sharing Sticklebricks*, page 116).

■ Allow plenty of time when it comes to helping children deal with disputes. If you are too quick to offer a solution, you will miss the opportunity to listen properly and help the children develop their understanding of what has happened.

■ Watch out for those children who always seem to win every argument. Emphasize the importance of sharing and give lots of praise when they are able to do so. At the same time, watch out for less dominant children and make sure they don't get passed over in a group.

■ Introduce strategies that encourage children to take turns (see *TRY THIS – strategies for sharing*). Introduce lots of co-operative activities (see *TRY THIS – co-operative activities*, page 116). Highlight occasions when children are co-operating and praise them for helping one another.

TRY THIS

Strategies for sharing

■ For child-initiated activities, limit numbers to three. Be flexible, though – if a larger group are playing well together, leave them to it.

■ For popular 'free choice time' activities such as easel painting, limit the queue to two or three children.

■ Check that children understand terminology such as 'wait', 'turn', 'share', 'join in'.

■ Introduce a special item during group discussion. When a child is holding the item it symbolizes that only they should speak and that everyone else should listen.

■ Use a timing device such as an egg timer during discussions or games. This gives each child the same length of time for their turn and shows children when their turn has ended.

■ Be firm about children respecting one another's activities. They can watch another child but not disturb or join in unless invited.

TRY THIS

Co-operative activities

- **Whispers:** put an item in a box. Whisper its name to the child sitting next to you and ask them to whisper the name to the next child. When the name has been whispered all round the circle, open the box to see if the name matches the object.

- **Circle massage:** seat the children in a line and show them how to massage one another's backs. Each child should ask their next-door neighbour whether they would like a back massage before proceeding (let children sit out if they prefer not to participate). Use different images to help them make appropriate movements: *'draw circles with your fists/make your fingers tap like raindrops.'*

- **Blindfold walk:** check that all the children are happy to wear blindfolds. Put them in pairs, blindfold one child and ask the other to lead them around the setting. Place a clean tissue inside the blindfold each time it is used.

- **Washing-up:** ask two children to wash and dry the snack time cups. Talk through how they are working together and helping each other.

SNAPSHOT – Sharing Sticklebricks

Cheng and Sara were playing with the Sticklebricks. When Cheng reached for the wheels, Sara also made a grab for them and the ensuing argument escalated until it came to the attention of their key worker. The key worker asked each child to explain the problem:

'Cheng has the wheels and I need them,' said Sara.

'But I had them first,' said Cheng.

The key worker asked the children to look in the box for some more wheels. When neither child was able to find alternative wheels, the key worker put the problem into words:

'You both want the same wheels but you can't use them at the same time. So – can you think what to do?'

'Take turns,' said Sara. The key worker asked Cheng what he thought and he agreed.

'So,' said the key worker, *'who had them first – who should have the first turn?'*

'Me,' said Cheng.

'But I saw them first,' shouted Sara.

The key worker intervened swiftly:

'I didn't see what happened but you will both have a turn. Cheng, you play with the wheels for five minutes and then Sara can have a turn for five minutes. Do you think that's a good idea?'

SNAPSHOT – continued

Cheng nodded and Sara said, 'OK – let's use the egg timer so I know if it's my turn.'
'Good idea, Sara,' said the key worker, before withdrawing and observing the children to make sure that they followed through with the solution. When both children had finished playing, the key worker praised them for sharing nicely.

This snapshot shoes the value of:

- Giving each child the opportunity to tell their version of the incident.
- Encouraging children to come up with their own solution to a dispute.
- Checking that both children agree with the solution.
- Observing to ensure that both children follow through with the solution, and praising them for doing so.

CURRICULUM GUIDANCE

Disagreements and sharing

Helping children to resolve disagreements contributes to many PSED goals, including:

Express needs and feelings in appropriate ways (green ss);

Have a developing awareness of their own needs, views and feelings and be sensitive to the needs, views and feelings of others (ELG);

Begin to accept the needs of others, with support (yellow ss);

Show confidence and the ability to stand up for own rights (green ss);

Consider the consequences of their words and actions for themselves and others (ELG).

Helping children to share contributes to many PSED goals, including:

Value and contribute to own well-being and self-control (green ss);

Work as part of a group … taking turns and sharing fairly, understanding that there needs to be agreed values and codes of behaviour for groups of people, including adults and children, to work together harmoniously (ELG).

Aggressive behaviour

Aggressive behaviour can be among the most difficult to deal with. Hitting, hair pulling and biting are just some of the aggressive acts that you will have to handle from time to time.

Strategies

- Encourage children to think of some alternatives: *'Instead of hitting Sayeed you could talk to him ... ask him "can I use the blue crayon when you've finished with it, Sayeed?"'*

- Comfort the victim and ensure they are not hurt. Although you must respond to the child who has been aggressive, avoid setting up a situation where aggressive behaviour is consistently rewarded with lots of attention.

- Decide whether to insist that children say sorry. Some settings hold the view that an enforced 'sorry' is meaningless, whereas others believe that learning to say sorry is an important social skill. If you do require children to say sorry, let their anger subside first and help them to understand the meaning of an apology.

- If negative behaviour persists, keep a child with you for a while. This gives them some 'time out' without making them feel isolated. Use your presence to calm the child and establish some boundaries, rather than rewarding their behaviour with attention. Give the child a simple explanation, such as: *'You can join your friends again when you are ready to share the Duplo'*.

- Aggressive behaviour should be dealt with immediately. As a last resort, use a holding technique to stop a child from hitting or kicking. When they are calm enough to listen, explain why they should not hit/kick/bite: *'We do not hit other people because it hurts them – and you don't want to hurt Christopher'*. Try appealing to their 'better nature': *'You're a kind girl, Cara, and kind girls don't hurt other people'*.

- If you feel that a child's aggressive behaviour is falling beyond normal parameters and may indicate special needs, consult with parents, follow your Special Needs policy and implement an Individual Education Plan (IEP) if necessary.

INFORMATION LINKS

For more on:

- anger, tantrums, aggressive behaviour and IEPs see pages 19–20 and Further reading.

CURRICULUM GUIDANCE

Aggressive behaviour

Helping children deal with aggression contributes to many PSED goals, including:

Have an awareness of the boundaries set and behavioural expectations within the setting (green ss);

Consider the consequences of their words and actions for themselves and others (ELG).

Tale telling and learning right from wrong

'Telling tales' is an outward sign that children are starting to make judgements about what constitutes appropriate behaviour.

Strategies

- ■ If dealing with 'tale telling' becomes wearing, remind yourself that it's a healthy stage in children's development. Give positive recognition when tale telling indicates an awareness that something shouldn't be happening and model how to deal with it. For example, when four-year-old Billy comes to tell you that a younger child is throwing sand, respond in a balanced way: *'Yes, Billy, Jessica shouldn't be throwing sand but she is still learning how to play safely in the sandpit. Let's go together and ask her not to throw sand.'*

- ■ When children come to you with a tale they are, in effect, asking you to sort things out. Help them to progress from simply noticing that something is amiss to addressing the problem. Ask the child: *'What can you do to help?'* Encourage them to come up with a solution and see it through.

- ■ Use everyday scenarios to help children explore 'right' and 'wrong': *'When you go to a party how do you behave?/When you go to the library how do you behave?'* Encourage children to think about the reasons for behaving in particular ways.

- ■ Helping children to realize that their behaviour impacts on others is essential to developing self control and the ability to function within a social group. Wherever possible, talk about how our actions affect others (see *SNAPSHOT – name calling*).

SNAPSHOT – name-calling

Staff had noticed that name-calling was escalating in the setting, with children picking up unpleasant words from one another. Together, they agreed on a policy to follow whenever the situation arose:

- ■ Recognize that younger children are simply imitating older ones and do not understand the consequences of their actions.

- ■ Respond by firmly asking the child not to use the unkind name and, if necessary, removing the child from the situation.

- ■ Protect the recipient's feelings by contradicting the child in tones of amazement: *'How strange that you should call Sanjit a horrid poo, Jessica – we all know that Sanjit is very kind and has lots of friends!'*

SNAPSHOT – continued

- Explain to older children that name-calling hurts a person's feelings. Ask them to think about how they would feel if they were called an unkind name.
- Without targeting specific children, use persona dolls, role play and stories to explore name-calling.

This snapshot shows the value of:

- *Picking up on repetitive negative behaviour through observation.*
- *Developing strategies as a team so that all staff are responding consistently.*

TRY THIS

Using picture books

A picture book is one of the best ways of helping children to explore relationships. Placing a friendship issue within the context of a story can make it much more meaningful to the child. You can also use the story to raise sensitive issues without focusing directly on a particular child. Try the following:

- *The Rainbow Fish*, Marcus Pfister (North-South Books) – friendship and sharing
- *Pumpkin Soup*, Helen Cooper (Corgi) – working together, quarrelling and making-up
- *I'm Sorry Sam*, McBratney (Picture Lions) – falling out, making-up and saying sorry
- *Can I Play?* Janet Thomas (Egmont Books) – being left out
- *Elmer: the Story of a Patchwork Elephant*, David Mc Kee (Red Fox) – accepting and valuing difference
- *Alfie Gives a Hand*, Shirley Hughes (Red Fox) – helping others.

Observation notes

Observation is the key to identifying and understanding patterns of behaviour within the setting:

- Use observation to help you decide when to intervene. Ideally, you should not step in too soon or you will deny children the chance to sort things out for themselves. At the same time, if you leave it too late, a minor situation could escalate into something more major.

■ Observe a child who persistently displays negative behaviour. Is the child's behaviour worse at certain times of the day, such as nearing home-time or during changes in routine? Is it better during adult-initiated activities or the less structured atmosphere of outdoor play? Give extra support and attention during 'trigger' moments and offer the child plenty of structure or carefully supervised freedom, depending on their needs.

■ When observing a child who struggles with relationships, look out for communication difficulties. Based on your observations, model appropriate social language and help the child practise how to say 'thank you', how to ask for something and so on. If you observe that the child's behaviour is having a negative effect, step in and help them to realize how much they are upsetting, disturbing or irritating others.

■ Use observation to help you discover which children are dominant and which children tend to get passed over or missed out during free play activities. Based on your observations, decide whether you need to step in and help redress the balance.

■ If you observe signs of social and behavioural difficulties that might indicate special needs, consult with parents and follow your Special Needs policy.

■ Observing children's behaviour may contribute to the following points in the **Foundation Profile** assessment scales:

– interacting with other children

Social development 1, 2, 3, 4, 5, 6, 7, 8, 9

Emotional development 3, 5, 6, 7, 8, 9

– how children handle disagreements and sharing

Social development 3, 4, 5, 6, 7, 8, 9

Emotional development 3, 5, 6, 7, 8, 9

– how children handle aggressive behaviour

Social development 7, 8

Emotional development 3, 5, 6, 7, 8, 9

– how children make moral decisions

Social development 3, 4, 5, 6, 7, 8, 9

Emotional development 4, 5, 6, 7, 8, 9

■ For examples of observation in practice, see SNAPSHOTS on pages 112, 113–14 and 116–7.

For a summary of different observational approaches, see page 4.

CURRICULUM GUIDANCE
Tale telling/learning right from wrong
Helping children develop moral awareness contributes to many PSED goals, including:

Show confidence and the ability to stand up for own rights (green ss);

Have an awareness of the boundaries set and behavioural expectations within the setting (green ss);

Understand what is right, what is wrong, and why (ELG).

The child in the physical setting

Young children's behaviour can have an impact on the physical environment as well as the other people in the setting. Helping children learn how to treat their surroundings with respect is an important aspect of behaviour management and essential to the child's development as a happy and functional human being.

Boisterous behaviour

Many children are naturally boisterous and it is essential that we do not squash their zest for life. However, most early years settings contain a large number of individuals and there does have to be some order if the setting is to function smoothly.
Strategies

- Offer the boisterous child as much physical play as possible. Ideally, they should have free access to the garden and you should provide an indoor climbing frame and soft play area during wet weather.

- Have some simple rules such as 'walking' and 'speaking quietly' when indoors. Help the children to explore what these rules mean in practice.

- Make sure the children understand the reasons for walking and speaking quietly in the setting. Use real life examples to show children how boisterous behaviour impacts both on other people and the physical surroundings.

- Banish negative terminology such as 'clumsy', 'careless' and 'noisy'. Instead of using negative labels and telling children what not to do, challenge them to behave appropriately: '*Show me how carefully you can carry the puzzle*' (see also *SNAPSHOT – quiet voices*, page 112).

■ Bear in mind that some children simply need to develop greater muscle strength and co-ordination. Set them lots of challenges, both to develop muscle control and heighten awareness of the need to be careful (see *TRY THIS – physical challenges,* page 124).

■ Playing with clay, washing walls and water painting provide boisterous children with some positive ways of channelling their extra energy.

■ Show children how to carry different objects (see *TRY THIS – carrying things*). Hold little groups to practise the techniques and, without making it too obvious, include boisterous children as often as possible.

■ Occasionally, children can be deliberately destructive. This is usually an expression of anger and you should respond accordingly:

  – intervene quickly;

  – once the child has calmed down, explain the reasons for not engaging in destructive behaviour;

  – involve the child in clearing up any mess;

  – if necessary, keep the child with you for 'time out'.

■ If you feel that a child has physical difficulties that fall beyond the normal parameters for their age, consult with parents and follow your Special Needs policy.

TRY THIS

Carrying things

Emphasize the importance of carrying just one thing at a time and show children techniques for carrying objects, for example:

■ **Carrying a chair:** show the children how to hold the seat of the chair so that it remains balanced with the legs pointing downwards.

■ **Carrying a tray:** show the children how to hold the middle of each side so that the tray is balanced.

■ **Carrying a large rolled floormat:** show the children how to wrap their arms around the middle of the roll and check that it is not trailing on the ground.

TRY THIS

Physical challenges

Apart from your planned physical development programme, there are lots of simple physical activities you can introduce on the spur of the moment. This will help boisterous children to expend their energy and develop muscular control and co-ordination:

- **Directed running:** ask children to run round the bushes or jump to the hedge before you finish counting to ten.

- **Balancing:** ask children to walk along a painted line or low wall – first walking normally, then heel to toe. As the children's physical control increases, challenge them to carry a hand bell without it ringing.

- **Putting objects down quietly:** challenge children to place a heavy object on the table without making a sound.

- **Pouring:** practise pouring jugs of dried beans (avoid toxic kidney beans and supervise closely). Progress to pouring liquids. Can the children fill their cups without spilling a drop?

CURRICULUM GUIDANCE

Boisterous behaviour

Helping children to conduct themselves appropriately within the setting contributes to many PSED goals, including:

Demonstrate flexibility and adapt their behaviour to different events, social situations and changes in routine (blue ss);

Have an awareness of the boundaries set and behavioural expectations within the setting (green ss);

Consider the consequences of their words and actions for themselves and others (ELG).

Helping children to control their movements within the setting contributes to many PD goals, including:

Show understanding of how to transport and store equipment safely (green ss);

Move with control and co-ordination (ELG);

Negotiate an appropriate pathway ... both indoors and outdoors (yellow ss);

Show respect for other children's personal space when playing among them (blue ss);

Show awareness of space, of themselves and of others (ELG).

Organizing physical space

If your setting is well organized, the children will find it much easier to function independently. When planning or reviewing the physical space in your setting, have the following aims in mind:

■ to enable children to function as independently as possible

■ to enable children to socialize freely

■ to enable children to move freely and in safety

■ to accommodate a range of activities, including quiet activities, boisterous activities, individual activities and 'messy play'

■ to provide a safe, comfortable and welcoming environment.

Observe how the children function within their physical space. If any areas seem problematic, look into re-organizing that part of the setting. The following checklist covers some of the elements you should consider:

■ Provide enough clear floor space for children to play on, preferably with a range of surfaces (carpet, smooth floor, matting).

■ Plan obstacle-free thoroughfares that do not pass through activity areas.

■ Check that you have a workable combination of open-plan and small, enclosed areas. Would more clear space be useful or does it tend to encourage over-boisterous play? Do your cosy areas become too cramped? Could you make them a little larger?

■ Think through the positioning of different areas of the setting – for example, locate the book corner away from the soft play area.

■ Check that different areas of the setting are designed for the children to use independently – for example, can children manage the toilet flush? Can they fix paper to the painting easel by themselves?

■ Provide plenty of freely available table space.

■ Enable children to 'mark out' their own activity areas with table mats and floor mats.

■ Display writing materials, books and other equipment so that they are easy to access and keep tidy.

- Set up child friendly storage systems for paintings, drawings and other 'work'. Ensure that coats, boots and lunchboxes are easy for the children to access.

- Use wipeable surfaces and plastic floor mats for water activities, painting and 'messy play'.

Establishing practical routines

Apart from providing a well-organized physical space, you need to introduce practical routines if the children are to function successfully within the setting. These will vary from setting to setting. The following checklist covers just some of the routines you might want to consider:

- putting away an activity when you have finished with it

- being careful with toys and equipment

- leaving play areas as you found them

- clearing up messes (see *TRY THIS – doing the housework*)

- tucking your chair under your table

- walking around someone working on a floor mat

- walking quietly indoors

- speaking quietly indoors

- limiting numbers in certain areas, for example, only three at a time in the play house (although you should be flexible if a larger group are playing well together)

- giving children responsibility for tidying the nature table/book corner/writing area.

TRY THIS

Doing the housework

Young children love clearing up messes, particularly when they have real equipment to use. Provide small dustpans and brushes, brooms, damp sponges, dusters, mops and buckets. Show the children how to use them and encourage them to take responsibility for 'doing the housework'.

INFORMATION LINKS

For more on:

■ introducing routines see page 16.

■ snacks, lunchtime and outdoor play routines see pages 86–9, 92–3, 94 and 107–8.

Observation notes

Use observation to find out how children are functioning within the physical setting. Observation is also essential for establishing whether different areas of the setting are supporting or hindering a child's learning and development:

■ As you observe children, look out for their level of physical co-ordination and how carefully they handle the equipment. Based on your observations, plan activities to support physical development and fill in any gaps (see *TRY THIS – carrying things*, page 123, for some examples). Your observations should also be used as the basis for planning activities to stretch the children (see *TRY THIS – physical challenges*, page 124, for some examples).

■ Track an individual child to see how they are using the available space and exploring the setting.

■ Position yourself near a specific area of the setting, such as the writing corner, and observe how it is used. Based on your observations, introduce changes if necessary to make the area more manageable for the children. Replace unpopular activities or come up with ways of making them more appealing.

■ Look out for signs of physical difficulties that may indicate special needs. Consult with parents, follow your Special Needs policy and implement an IEP if necessary.

■ Observing children as they interact with the physical setting may contribute to the following points in the **Foundation Profile** assessment scales:
  – how children conduct themselves within the physical setting

    Social development 4, 5, 6, 7

    Emotional development 5, 7, 8
  – how children manage routines within the setting

    Dispositions and attitudes 3, 5
  – how children move within the setting

    Physical development 1, 2, 3, 4, 5.

For a summary of different observational approaches, see page 4.

CURRICULUM GUIDANCE

Organizing physical space/establishing routines

A well-organized physical space helps children to operate more independently. This contributes to a number of PSED goals, including:

Show increasing independence in selecting and carrying out activities (blue ss);

Operate independently within the environment ... (green ss);

Select and use activities independently (ELG).

Sound practical routines help children learn how to conduct themselves in the setting. This contributes to a number of PSED goals, including:

Work as part of a group ... understanding that there needs to be agreed values and codes of behaviour for groups of people including adults and children to work together harmoniously (ELG);

Show care and concern for others, for living things and the environment (blue ss);

Have an awareness of the boundaries set and behavioural expectations within the setting (green ss);

Understand what is right, what is wrong, and why (ELG).

A well-organized physical space and sound practical routines help children develop the ability to move appropriately within the setting. This contributes to many PD goals, including:

Move freely with pleasure and confidence (blue ss);

Move with confidence, imagination and in safety (ELG);

Negotiate an appropriate pathway when walking ... both indoors and outdoors (yellow ss);

Show respect for other children's personal space when playing among them (blue ss);

Show awareness of space, of themselves and of others (ELG).

The adult's role

You and your colleagues are the most important resource in the early years setting. Everything, from the physical surroundings to the nature of adult/child relationships, is down to you! While there is no such thing as the perfect practitioner, we can all aspire to be 'good enough'.

Doing a 'self-audit'

A regular, self-motivated check on how you function in the setting will help you to develop your skills. Think about your attitudes, values, assumptions, practices and how you relate to and handle the children. The following checklist includes some areas to consider:

- Always remember that you are part of a team. Your work will be so much more enjoyable if you and your colleagues can appreciate one another's strengths, share triumphs and disasters and support one another with generosity. If you are inexperienced, you can learn a huge amount from colleagues. If you are a setting manager, take seriously your role as a mentor to inexperienced staff.

- Aim to present a united front to the children. Give support if a colleague is having difficulties; at the same time, try not to take over unless a child's safety is at stake (see *SNAPSHOT – supporting a colleague*, page 131).

- Ask yourself if you truly care about each child. Although you may struggle to like every child in the group, you should still have their best interests at heart. If you try hard enough, you can usually find something positive in every child.

- Never forget that you are a role model and that the children will imitate you. Try to abide by the same rules as the children and don't be afraid to apologize to a child if you get something wrong or make a mistake.

- Check tone of voice, body language and vocabulary (see *TRY THIS – colleague observation*). Analyse a tricky scenario while it's still fresh in your mind. Could you have used more positive terminology? Was your body language threatening, even though your words were kind? Did you shout or show anger? If anger is a problem, try some calming strategies such as a relaxation technique.

TRY THIS

Colleague observation

Ask a colleague to observe you handling a situation with a child. Ask them to check your tone of voice, body language and use of words. Choose a colleague you feel relaxed with and ask them to be honest! The process might feel more comfortable if you can reciprocate by observing them back.

- Try to move unobtrusively in the setting. This doesn't mean squashing your personality if you are naturally exuberant – simply be careful not to disturb or distract children who are concentrating.

- Aim to start every day afresh. We are all programmed to make assumptions about others and base our expectations on previous experience. This can be counterproductive for young children, who can so easily become labelled as 'naughty', 'shy' or 'destructive'. Ask yourself whether your expectations about certain children might be trapping them in a negative cycle of behaviour.

- Try not to take things personally – remember that the children are still learning how to relate to other people (see *SNAPSHOT – a thick skin*, page 19). If there are home difficulties, keep reminding yourself of how much pressure the child is under.

- Remember that young children do not always give the same feedback as adults. It can be surprising when a parent tells you what an impression you have made on a child you thought was beyond your reach. Have faith that you *will* have a positive impact if you keep on doing all the right things.

- Regard negative behaviour as a challenge. Anyone can work with the 'easy' child, but the one who presents lots of problems will really help you develop your skills as an early years practitioner.

- Always try to see things through (see *SNAPSHOT – supporting a colleague*, page 131). It can be tempting to 'avoid' challenging behaviour, particularly when a child turns tail and runs at the sight of you (it happens to everyone at some point!) Don't give up, though. If you keep persisting, you will usually get through in the end.

- Check whether you encourage children to make their own choices and sort out problems independently, rather than leaping in at the first possible moment. Of course, there are always times when you have to clear that table or get those coats on – but whenever possible, let children do things for themselves.

- Avoid talking about the children when they are present. Quite apart from the fact that they pick up far more than we think, it shows a lack of respect for the child.

- Work at becoming aware of all the children, even when you are dealing with just one. Developing 'eyes in the back of your head' is an important skill for any teacher, and one to be proud of.

- Seek support if you feel your relationship with a child has deteriorated to a point where the child may suffer. Don't feel a failure! Asking for help means that you are putting the child first, which is the professional thing to do.

- Don't beat yourself up if you have a bad day – everyone has them. After all, how can you help children to take a positive attitude and learn from their mistakes if you don't allow yourself to do the same?

SNAPSHOT – supporting a colleague

The setting manager was observing Ellie, an inexperienced practitioner, as she tried to get Nicky to put away his cars. He had run off to the other side of the room and Ellie was clearly unsure of what to do next. The setting manager approached her and said:

'You need to follow this up – Nicky can be very determined. Go over to him, get down to his level and insist that he puts away his toys. I'll support you if necessary.'

Ellie went over to Nicky, knelt down and said as firmly as she could:

'Nicky, come and put away your cars please.'

This time, Nicky did not run away, but he still refused to co-operate.

'Come on, I'll help you,' said Ellie.

Still Nicky refused to move. The setting manager came across and said:

'Miss Ellie, it's Nicky's turn on the climbing frame. Can he go outside when he's tidied away his toys?'

'Yes,' said Ellie, *'come on Nicky, when you've put away your cars you can go outside.'*

Nicky looked at Ellie and the setting manager said to him:

'Miss Ellie will watch you put away all the cars and then she'll take you to the cloakroom so you can put on your coat.'

Nicky nodded and went off with Ellie. Later in the day, the setting manager reassured Ellie that the children would gradually stop challenging her as they came to realize that she would always follow a situation through.

This snapshot shows the value of:

- *Following through a strategy to deal with challenging behaviour, however tempted you are to give up and walk away.*
- *Drawing on support from a more experienced colleague when necessary.*
- *Giving support to a less experienced colleague, without undermining their authority.*
- *Offering a child an enticing experience to encourage the desired behaviour. (Nicky is given the implicit message that the sooner he puts away his cars, the sooner he can go outside.)*

TRY THIS

A mental note

As a part of your 'self audit', make a list of things you want to work on. This might include:

■ giving children time to sort out a situation by themselves before intervening

■ becoming more aware of what is happening throughout the setting

■ using non- threatening body language when communicating with children.

Make a mental note of the particular aspect you want to focus on for that day. Be sure to write down your successes at the end of the session – and give yourself a pat on the back!

A behaviour policy

Formulating a behaviour policy is an essential aspect of the practitioner's role. A behaviour policy gives all the adults in the setting a common structure to follow, as well as providing parents and outside agencies with written information on how you support behaviour. The actual process of formulating the policy also offers a useful opportunity to assess your approach to supporting behaviour. All staff should be involved in its formulation and the policy should be revised on a regular basis. The children should also be involved with formulating their own rules (see *Rules* below). Although the policy for each setting will differ, the following framework covers the main areas to consider:

■ **Overall aim:** to provide a caring environment where children are encouraged to respect themselves, others and their surroundings.

■ **Responsibility for behaviour:** name the person responsible for overseeing behavioural issues, keeping up-to-date with research and legislation and organizing appropriate staff training.

■ **Rules (for everyone in the setting):**

–   we are kind and helpful to others

–   we never hurt others

–   we do not use unkind words

–   we look after our setting

–   we look after our pets and plants

–   we clear away after ourselves

–   we do not interrupt or spoil other people's activities.

■ Approaches to supporting behaviour: all staff act as role models, treating each other and the children with courtesy, patience and kindness. We teach by example and have positive and consistent expectations of all children. Staff always aim to:

- praise acceptable behaviour

- explain reasons for intervening when behaviour is unacceptable

- focus on what children *should* be doing, rather than what they *shouldn't* be doing

- avoid giving negative labels

- where appropriate, give children 'time out' by requiring them to stay with an adult

- encourage children to make good any damage caused (in a child-appropriate manner)

- recognize that behavioural codes vary from culture to culture and respect these differences

- use holding techniques only where absolutely necessary to prevent children from injuring themselves or others

- work in partnership with parents, involving them fully in addressing any behavioural problems.

Staff do not:

- leave a child alone

- use physical punishment such as smacking

- single out or humiliate a child

- shout, use raised voices or aggressive language

- use threatening behavour.

■ **Special needs**: when a child's behavioural difficulties arise from special needs, we follow our Special Needs policy, acting in full consultation with parents and, if necessary, outside support agencies to design and implement an Individual Education Plan (IEP).

■ **Bullying:** we define bullying as the persistent and deliberate abuse of a child. We keep a close eye out for bullying and, where necessary, respond with the following strategies:

- intervention to protect the bullied child

- reassurance to the bullied child

- an explanation to the child doing the bullying why their behaviour is unacceptable

- praise when the child doing the bullying shows appropriate behaviour

- full parental involvement in dealing with situations of bullying

- avoidance of the label 'bully'.

Further reading and references

Bayley, Ros (2005) *Exploring Emotions*. Leamington Spa: Step Forward Publishing.
(Helping children explore emotions using stories, puppets, toys, pictures and games.)

Clarke, Jennie (2005) *Snack Time: Establishing Healthy Eating for Life Through Snack Time in the Early Years*. Lutterworth: Featherstone Education.

Cumine, Val, Leach, Julie and Stevenson, Gill (2000) *Autism in the Early Years: A Practical Guide*. London: David Fulton Publishers.

Drifte, Collette (2002) *Special Needs in Early Years Settings: A Practitioner's Guide*. London: David Fulton Publishers.

Drifte, Collette (2004) *Encouraging Positive Behaviour in the Early Years: A Practical Guide*. London: Paul Chapman Publishing.
(Useful information on the 2001 SEN code of practice, implementing a positive behaviour policy and Individual Education Plans.)

Dunant, Sue (2004) *Outdoor Play*. Leamington Spa: Step Forward Publishing.
(Ideas for making the most of outdoor facilities, however limited your space.)

Featherstone, Sally (2003) *The Little Book of Outside in All Weathers*. Lutterworth: Featherstone Education.

Holland, Penny (2003) *We Don't Play with Guns Here: War, Weapons and Superhero Play in the Early Years*. Maidenhead: Open University Press.
(Positive approaches to handling apparently aggressive play.)

Hutchin, Vicky (2003) *Observing and Assessing for the Foundation Stage Profile*. London: Hodder and Stoughton.
(Useful survey of observation/assessment methods and how they can be used to complete the statutory Foundation Stage Profile.)

Mortimer, Hannah (2002) *Supporting Children with AD/HD and Attention Difficulties in the Early Years*. Stafford: QEd Publications.

Mosley, Jenny and Sonnet, Helen (2005) *Here We Go Round: Quality Circle Time for 3 to 5 Year Olds*. Trowbridge: Positive Press.
(Circle time activities to help develop confidence and listening, thinking and speaking skills.)

OFSTED (2001) *Full Day Care: Guidance to the National Standards*. London: DfES.
(Handbook for the National Standards that OFSTED expect from all day care providers.)

Portwood, Madeleine (1999) *Developmental Dyspraxia: Identification and Intervention*. London: David Fulton Publishers.

Pre-school Learning Alliance (2005) *Policies for Early Years Settings*. London: Pre-school Learning Alliance.
(Sample policies covering everything from special needs to food and drink.)
QCA (2003) *The Foundation Stage Profile Handbook*. London: Qualifications and Curriculum Authority.
Welford, Heather (2002) *Successful Potty Training*. London: National Childbirth Trust.
(Includes information on supporting children with special needs.)

Index

0 1341 1057024 6

2008 02 05